EXPLORING
THE LIFE, MYTH, AND ART OF
ANCIENT ROME

CIVILIZATIONS OF THE WORLD

EXPLORING the LIFE, MYTH, and ART of ANCIENT ROME

TONY ALLAN

ROSEN
PUBLISHING®

New York

This edition published in 2012 by:

The Rosen Publishing Group, Inc.
29 East 21st Street
New York, NY 10010

Additional end matter copyright © 2012 by The Rosen Publishing Group, Inc.

Cover design by Nelson Sá

Library of Congress Cataloging-in-Publication Data

Allan, Tony, 1946-
Exploring the life, myth, and art of ancient Rome/Tony Allan.
    p. cm.—(Civilizations of the world)
Includes bibliographical references and index.
ISBN 978-1-4488-4831-7 (library binding)
1. Rome—Social life and customs—Juvenile literature. 2. Mythology, Roman—Juvenile literature. 3. Art, Roman—Juvenile literature. 4. Rome—Civilization—Juvenile literature. 5. Rome—History—Empire, 30 B.C.-476 A.D.—Juvenile literature. I. Title.
DG78.A54 2012
937—dc22

2011009799

Manufactured in the United States of America

CPSIA Compliance Information: Batch #S11YA: For further information, contact Rosen Publishing, New York, New York, at 1-800-237-9932.

Copyright © Duncan Baird Publishers
Text © Tony Allan
Commissioned artworks and map © Duncan Baird Publishers

CONTENTS

IMAGE AND IMAGINATION

A t first sight, the story of Rome seems more the stuff of fantasy or legend than of history. It tells how the inhabitants of a small town and its hinterland—a region with few obvious natural or strategic advantages—managed, by military prowess, to make themselves masters first of Italy and then of the entire Mediterranean world, including much of Europe, the Middle Eastern area, and North Africa. Only the Han Chinese (206BCE–220CE), the Romans' contemporaries far away in the unknown east, could in any way rival their achievement. Yet there was always more to Rome's progress than simple skill in arms. The Romans were also builders and law-makers on a heroic scale, and they left a permanent mark on all the lands that they ruled.

THE SOUL OF THE ROMANS

Anyone seeking to understand the Romans should start with their military background. First and foremost, they were good and valiant soldiers. Initially, they fought out of necessity, to ensure the survival of their remote and hilly city. Later, the urge for expansion entered their bloodstream—victory in repeated doses turned out to be a heady drug.

In the days when the Romans were conquering Italy (ca. 500–246BCE), their soldiers were peasant smallholders who, when duty demanded, abandoned their plows and took up the sword. This situation changed from about 100BCE on, when the consul Marius created a professional standing army of long-serving legionaries. Yet well after the citizens' army had faded into history, citizens looked back admiringly to the days of a patriotic yeomanry fighting for hearth and home and continued, above all, to respect such soldierly virtues as duty, hardiness, and courage.

Needless to say, not all Romans exhibited these admirable qualities, and, in its later years, the Empire gained an enduring reputation for decadence and luxury. Even so, moralists regularly harked back to the traditions of earlier, republican times. Meanwhile, the mass of the population continued to harbor one essential ingredient of the military spirit: an ingrained respect for authority. Discipline and order were essential parts of the Roman worldview. Such attributes extended beyond a respect for those who wielded political power at any given moment. They also included the concepts of *pietas*, or piety, demanding respectful observance toward the gods and the state,

LEFT A statue from the mid-1st century CE depicting a figure holding the busts of his forefathers. Such forceful patriarchal images were an expression of the respect for authority and hierarchy that was so central to Roman ideology and that penetrated every sphere of human life. The *paterfamilias*, or father of the family, was the undisputed head of the household—his supreme power over it extended to legal jurisdiction.

RIGHT A relief panel from the *Ara Pacis* ("Altar of Peace") commissioned by the Senate on Augustus's return from Spain and Gaul in 13BCE. The panel, an allegory of Italy's renewed fertility following the *Pax Augusta* ("Peace of Augustus"), depicts Terra Mater, or Mother Earth, with two babies. Although women were perceived as subordinate figures in the strongly paternalistic Roman world, they nevertheless had greater legal rights than their counterparts in Greece and could, in private, exert considerable influence.

and *gravitas*, seriousness, which implied self-discipline and the need for a sober approach to life.

In time, Roman rule spread so wide that its Romanness—the quality called at the time *Romanitas*—was inevitably diluted. The Empire became a multiethnic community whose emperors included Africans, a Syrian, and an Arab; its arts came mainly from Greece and its religions increasingly from the Orient. Yet a kernel of the old traditions always remained. From it came the Romans' most enduring legacy: the practical and intellectual skills that won battles, shaped cities, and developed a legal system that is still influential in many parts of the world today. Such achievements helped bind the Empire together and continued to affect distant peoples long after the demise of the western emperors in 476CE.

THE STORY OF THE ROMANS

The story of the greatest empire of the ancient world begins with shepherds living in wattle-and-daub huts roofed with thatch on the Palatine Hill early in the first millennium BCE. Similar groups established villages on adjoining hills. At some point, traditionally dated to 753BCE but more likely in the following century, the various settlements coalesced to form the city of Rome.

The remaining thousand years of Roman history can best be summarized in six phases of varying length (see timeline, page 136). The first such was the Etruscan period, lasting through the sixth century BCE. The Etruscans were a people who had settled the region now known as Tuscany immediately to the north of Rome. They grew rich on trade and the profits of mining and used this wealth to finance a lavish lifestyle in which the arts flourished. Politically, they never coalesced; Etruria remained a world of independent city-states.

When a line of Etruscan kings established themselves as rulers of Rome sometime between 625 and 600BCE, the burgeoning community was effectively incorporated into an expanded Etruria. After more than a century of domination, the last Etruscan king, Tarquin the Proud, was expelled in about 509BCE, and a republic was set up to replace the monarchy. Later generations of Romans looked back on Tarquin's ousting as a liberation.

The next period, covering the years from approximately 500 to 246BCE, was the time of the conquest of Italy. This era saw Rome's power spread out from its home region of Latium (hence "Latin") over the neighboring Italian peoples, including the city's erstwhile masters, the Etruscans. This was a time that later writers would look back on as the golden age of republican virtue, when honor, courage, and a sense of civic duty impelled the nation to greatness.

LEFT A double-edged Roman *gladius*, or short sword (27in/68cm long), with scabbard. Rome's military supremacy lay in its effectiveness at conducting land warfare, with the short sword being a highly effective stabbing weapon in the close-quarters crush of battle. Other standard fighting equipment of the legionaries included the *pilum*, a spear, and the *scutum*, a long shield.

Last to fall were the sophisticated city-states of southern Italy, settled by Greek colonists many centuries before. The Greeks called for help on Pyrrhos, ruler of Epiros across the Adriatic Sea. The Greek invader inflicted several defeats on the Romans, but many of his men were lost in battle—these were the original Pyrrhic victories, bought at an unsustainable cost. When Pyrrhos eventually returned to Greece in 275BCE, he left the path clear for Rome to make itself master of the Italian peninsula south of the Po River. (The Celts, who lived north of the Po in the region known as Cisalpine Gaul, did not come under Roman control until 150BCE.)

The years from the mid-third to the mid-second century BCE were dominated by the struggle with Carthage, the great trading center set up by Phoenicians many centuries earlier on the North African coast. Three great conflicts—the Punic Wars—set the two rivals at one another's throats. When Rome finally emerged victorious in 146BCE, it precluded the possibility of any further challenge by totally demolishing Carthage and plowing over its ruins, sowing salt in the furrows to ensure that nothing would grow on the site for many years.

The Punic Wars radically changed Rome. First, they turned it into a Mediterranean power whose naval strength came to match its military might. Then they

RIGHT A detail from the Lyons Tablet, a monumental inscription in bronze of the text of emperor Claudius's speech to the Senate in ca. 48CE, proposing the extension of citizenship to the leading men of the tribes of Gaul. Following his annexation of Britain in 43CE, this speech formed part of Claudius's attempt to establish good relations between Gaul and Rome. The speech was so well received in Gaul that it became monumentalized in this tablet, only half of which has survived.

made it rich through its domination of the great trade routes of the Mediterranean world. Finally, victory against Carthage, and also against such other enemies of the day as Illyria, Macedonia, and Asia Minor, brought slaves to Italy by the tens of thousands in the form of prisoners of war. From that time on, slaves replaced the hardy farmers of early Rome as the economic foundation of the state.

The next epoch of Roman history was a transitional one, marking the crucial shift from republic to empire. This was a time of high political drama whose leading players—Julius Caesar, Cicero, Pompey, Brutus, Mark Antony—remain familiar names to this day. Against a backdrop of social unrest and slave revolts—Spartacus held out with his army of gladiators from 73 to 71BCE—real power passed from Rome's republican institutions to a succession of military strong men. From this time on, the legions became the true arbiters of Roman power.

The logical culmination of this process came in 27BCE, when Augustus, Rome's first emperor, assumed power. Henceforth, the nation would be ruled by the supreme commander of the army, and the old republican institutions of consuls and the Senate were restricted to a strictly advisory role. The limitations of the imperial model soon became apparent with the appearance of the third emperor, Caligula, who famously made his favorite horse a consul and was almost certainly clinically insane. The instability inherent in a regime based on military approval was also vividly illustrated in 69CE, the "Year of the Four Emperors," when two rulers were murdered and a third committed suicide under pressure from the legions.

Yet for all the confusion of the late republican and early imperial periods, the Empire itself continued to grow. Greece had become a Roman province in 146BCE; Gaul (modern France and Belgium) was conquered by Julius Caesar between 58 and 51 BCE; Egypt was annexed by Augustus; the emperor Claudius oversaw the conquest of what is now England and Wales from 43CE. The last great burst of

RIGHT The map shows the Roman Empire at its greatest extent during the 2nd century CE under the emperor Trajan, following Rome's nearly 500-year-old policy of steady territorial expansion. By Trajan's death in 117CE, the Empire had 40 provinces—from Hispania Terraconensis, Lusitania, and Baetica (modern Spain) in the west to Judaea and Syria in the eastern Mediterranean, and Britannia in the north to the rich provinces of North Africa in the south— in total encompassing an area of some 2 million square miles (5 million square kilometers).

CALEDONIA

HIBERNIA

BRITANNIA
● Londinium

Seine River

Rhine River

BELGICA
Trier ●
GERMANIA

GAUL

Dordogne River

Lyons ●

HISPANIA

LUSITANIA

BAETICA
● Córdoba
● Cádiz

Tangier ●

MAURETANIA

CORSICA

SARDINIA

Milan ●
Ravenna ●

ITALIA

Rome ●
Naples ●

*Tyrrhenean
Sea*

Carthage ●

Dougga ●

NUMIDIA

SICILY

DACIA

Danube River

ILLYRIA

*Adriatic
Sea*

MACEDONIA

THRACIA

ACHAEA
Athens ●
*Aegean
Sea*

CRETE

● Ephesus

Black Sea

● Constantinople

ASIA MINOR

CYPRUS

Caspian Sea

ARMENIA

Tigris River

PARTHIA

Antioch ●

Euphrates River

SYRIA

Mediterranean Sea

Cyrene ●

CYRENAICA

Alexandria ●

Memphis ●

EGYPT

JUDAEA
● Jerusalem

Nile River

SCALE

0   500   1,000 km

0   250   500 miles

N

KEY

Roman empire at its
greatest extent in the
early 2nd century CE.

imperial expansion took place under Trajan, who added Dacia (modern Transylvania), Armenia, and Mesopotamia early in the second century CE. The last two conquests turned out to represent the high-water mark of the Empire and were abandoned by Trajan's successor, Hadrian, who introduced a new, enduring policy of preserving what Rome already had rather than reaching out for more.

Trajan and Hadrian, as it happens, feature as the second and third of the "Five Good Emperors"—a succession of able rulers (the first was Nerva, the fourth and fifth Antoninus Pius and the philosopher Marcus Aurelius) who provided the Empire with almost a century of efficient and stable government between 96 and 180CE. This fifth phase was the imperial heyday, when the vast majority of the Empire's peoples could go about their business undisturbed beneath the shelter of the *Pax Romana* ("Roman Peace"). Life was comfortable and cosmopolitan, at least for the wealthy; great feats of engineering were achieved, particularly in road-building, and education spread widely.

LEFT The Forum Romanum, or Roman Forum (see pages 28–29), consisted of a series of public buildings conceived as an expression of state power. This relief from the Arch of Titus in the Forum shows a procession of triumphant Roman soldiers returning from the conquest of Jerusalem in 70CE. Spoils from the Temple of Jerusalem, including a seven-branched candelabrum, are being carried by the soldiers.

Yet the Empire was always under threat, from the insidious dangers of inflation and corruption within its borders and from the pressure of the foreign enemies the Romans called barbarians without (see pages 50–51). In its final phase, which ended in the collapse of the western Empire, it gradually succumbed. The process was slow—almost three centuries passed between the death of Marcus Aurelius and the abdication of the last western emperor in 476CE—and the decline was by no means unrelieved. These years saw the triumph of Christianity and the establishment of the eastern Roman Empire, which would survive for more than a millennium before its capital, Constantinople, finally fell to the Ottoman Turks in 1453. For the western Empire, though, there was no such reprieve. Rome itself was sacked by Goths in 410CE, and, under continued barbarian onslaught, the structures of imperial government that had been so lengthily and laboriously constructed were gradually pulled down.

BELOW A mosaic (ca. 500CE) from Carthage shows a horseman in Germanic dress. The "barbarian" Germanic peoples who settled in North Africa wished to share in the wealth of Rome, and they adopted many of the trappings of Roman life when acquiring control.

THE ETRUSCAN HERITAGE

In its early days, Rome grew up in the shadow of its wealthier northern neighbors, the city-states of Etruria, and inherited many elements of its civilization from them (see page 10). An enduring part of the heritage was a taste for beautiful things. For at a time when the inhabitants of Rome were still unpolished provincials, the Etruscans were already producing impressive works of art, such as the examples shown here: a magnificent bronze statuette, ca. 300–280BCE, a pair of gold earrings, 525–500BCE (above), and an exquisite bronze dish handle, 350–300BCE, in the form of a nude, winged girl (opposite).

THE ART OF ROME

For those accustomed to thinking in terms of national schools of painting and sculpture, Roman art remains something of an enigma. In truth, it barely existed, if the term is taken to mean work produced by Italian artists in a purely Roman style. Instead, the body of work that goes under that label was always supranational in its inspiration as well as its creative talent. In the early years, it was almost entirely derivative, partly from Etruscan models, but mostly from the Greeks. Later, however, Roman art developed into something altogether more original and is recognizable to the modern eye as an international classical style. Although still taking its inspiration largely from Greece, Roman art forms extended their influence around the entire Mediterranean world and traveled wherever the legions carried the standards of Rome.

Like so much else, the taste for Greek art came to Rome initially among the spoils of war. The conquest first of the Greek cities of southern Italy and Sicily, then of Greece itself, and finally of Hellenistic Asia Minor in the course of the third and second centuries BCE, flooded Rome with pillaged artworks. Greek artists followed, eager to cater to the craze for all things Hellenic that swept through the wealthy classes. The vogue stretched to imitations as well as original pieces, and soon Rome supported a flourishing mini-industry producing copies of masterworks by great Greek sculptors of earlier times.

LEFT **This magnificent Roman marble statue (ca. 125CE)—in imitation of Greek sculpture and by an unknown artist—is of the Greek god Herakles (Roman Hercules). It was one of numerous similar pieces commissioned by the emperor Hadrian (reigned 117–138CE), whose love of Hellenism led him to be nicknamed "the Greekling." The statue was found in 1790, near the ruins of Hadrian's villa at Tivoli (see illustration pages 22–23).**

Nevertheless, Roman art gradually developed distinctive features. One was a taste for warts-and-all realism, most marked in certain Roman portrait busts and in a series of remarkable sarcophagi (elaborate coffins) sculpted for private clients in imperial times. Although the sculptors were themselves often Greeks living in Italy, the patrons they worked for evidently accepted or even demanded a greater degree of fidelity to nature than their counterparts on the other side of the Adriatic Sea.

A similar adherence to a new set of ideals and conventions informed another Roman artform, the commemorative relief. The earliest examples date from around 100BCE, but the finest are from the imperial period. None has stood the test of time better than the lengthy frieze that snakes up Trajan's Column in Rome (see illustration, right).

Painting for the Romans typically meant wall decoration, and art historians now distinguish four separate styles covering the period from roughly 100BCE to 200CE. The first did little more than imitate marble blocks, while the second favored elaborate architectural vistas. In the Augustan age (27BCE–14CE), a third style featuring central panels depicting mythological or pastoral scenes came into vogue, giving way in its turn to a fourth, baroque style that flanked the panels with fantastic perspective effects and fanciful arabesques.

Mural painting fell into decline from the start of the third century CE, by which time some genres of Roman art were being transformed significantly. Classical art in general was giving way to the style now known as Late Antique. Over the next 300 years, the idealized humanism of the Greek tradition would finally fade away, to be replaced by the God-centered priorities of medieval art.

RIGHT **A section from the 640-feet-long (200-metre) frieze on Trajan's Column in Rome, erected in celebration of Trajan's victories against the Dacians between 101 and 106CE. The laws of perspective have sometimes been deliberately overruled to create a nonstop panorama of an army in action, cramming some 2,500 individual figures into a single, continuous narrative of conquest.**

THE ARCHITECTURE OF ROME

O f all the visual arts, architecture best suited the Roman character. Massive construction in stone and brick played to the Romans' talent for organization and to their engineering strengths, and also catered to their rulers' love of display. The remains of many of their great public buildings still stand to this day, mutely testifying to the grandeur that was Rome.

As with much of Rome's artistic inheritance, a considerable amount of the initial impetus came from the Greeks, mediated through Etruscan influences. By historic times, wealthy Romans were living in villas that closely resembled those of Greece or, more precisely, those of the Greek colonists of southern Italy. The town houses preserved at Pompeii and Herculaneum have blank walls giving onto the street in the manner of their equivalents in Sybaris or Syracuse. Inside, rooms radiate off the atrium, a central hall that, unlike its Greek counterpart, was usually covered. However, larger villas often also incorporated an uncovered courtyard in the Greek manner, pleasantly decorated with flowers and artworks, and perhaps with a fountain to provide a constant murmur of running water.

Most of the more familiar Roman monuments date not from republican but imperial times, when Rome's rulers had the money for major projects. A golden age of Roman architecture extended between the reigns of Nero and Hadrian, from 54 to 138CE, although there was an earlier surge of construction under Augustus and later revivals under such rulers as Caracalla, Diocletian, and Constantine.

The Romans' greatest technical contribution lay in the development of concrete, which was introduced in the second century BCE. Although marble was also widely used in Roman public building, concrete became the material of choice for large-scale construction by the end of the following century. The finest concrete

RIGHT A view of the Arch of Constantine looking toward via San Gregorio, Rome. Situated between the Palatine Hill and the Colosseum, this triumphal arch was erected ca. 315CE to commemorate Constantine's victory over Maxentius in the battle for control of the western Empire at the Milvian Bridge in 312CE. The structure's three white marble archways are flanked by Corinthian columns, four on each side of the building, which stand on plinths.

was made of lime and water mixed with the special soil known as *pozzolana*, so called because the principal deposits were found at Pozzuoli, near Naples. *Pozzolana* was a mix of clay and volcanic cinders that gained great strength when combined with an aggregate of rubble—often the chippings from builders' masonry.

Concrete freed up building techniques when combined with another defining feature of Roman architecture—the semicircular arch. This innovation came originally from Greece by way of the Etruscans, who had first realized that a central keystone, held in place by wedge-shaped supporting stones called *voussoirs*, could create a solid framework for construction. When poured into molds held in place between a skeleton of arches, concrete could be shaped into domes, apses, niches, and vaults, opening up large areas of floor space by reducing the need for pillars and other supports.

Concrete in combination with the arch provided the technological underpinning for the wave of public building that marked early imperial days. One typical structure of the time was the basilica, usually oblong in shape with a semicircular apse at the far end, and with twin rows of columns separating the central hallway from parallel side aisles. For the early Romans, the basilica was part law court, part municipal building. In later years, it was adopted by Christians as a template for church-building.

Yet it is the bigger, more grandiose structures for which the Romans are best remembered: triumphal arches, victory columns, theaters, and amphitheaters

such as the Colosseum in Rome, built to seat around 50,000 spectators (see pages 86–87). Architects may have been brought up to respect order and harmony by writers like Vitruvius, whose handbook of architecture, written in Augustus's reign, was to have huge influence when rediscovered more than a millennium later by the builders of Renaissance Italy. What their patrons sought, however, was splendor and massive grandeur—unmistakable icons of Roman power. To Rome's Dark Age successors, such structures seemed the work of giants, and they still impress by their size and magnificence to the present day.

THE ROMAN WORLD

LEFT The Ephesus Library
was built in 135CE in
Ephesus (modern-day
Turkey) by Julius Aquila,
in honor of his father,
Celsus Polemaeanus of
Sardis, a Roman senator
and proconsul of the
province of Asia. The first
public library in Rome was
opened in the 1st century
BCE, and, by the 2nd century
CE, there were said to be
twenty-five in the capital
alone. Such initiatives
encouraged the spread
of literacy throughout
the Empire and also,
crucially, facilitated the
promotion of Roman
culture and ideology in
its far-flung provinces.

I n its heyday, the Roman Empire was a vast, multinational power that brought together peoples of many different races and religions in a single grand endeavor. In some ways, Romanization even foreshadowed the globalization of recent times. On the streets of Rome, native Italians rubbed shoulders with Greeks, Syrians, North Africans, Spaniards, Gauls, Celts, and Germans, among many others. Yet the whole enterprise rested ultimately on insecure foundations—on conquest and slavery. The Roman world was one of winners and losers, whose harsh contrasts were mirrored in the mingled grandeur and squalor of the city of Rome itself.

BELOW A fragment from the
Forma Urbis Romae, a large
(ca. 60 feet x 43 feet / ca. 18
meter x 13 meter) ground
plan of ancient Rome.
Carved in marble at the
beginning of the 3rd
century CE, the map records
in astounding detail every
architectural feature of the
city, from large monuments
and major streets to shops,
taverns, alleys, rooms, and
even staircases. Only 10 to
15 percent of the original
map remains.

THE ETERNAL CITY

At the height of its imperial power, Rome was the wonder of the world. A million or more people lived in its crowded streets. The city had been so generously endowed by its rulers that almost half the available space in the central districts was taken up by civic buildings. The most impressive of its monuments were unmatched for grandeur anywhere in the world, and their memory lingers to this day: names like the Capitol, the Colosseum, and the Circus Maximus still resonate. The greatest structures in terms of sheer size were the public bath complexes. The stately architecture was matched by an engineering infrastructure of unparalleled sophistication in which the city's water supply took pride of place.

Splendid though its monuments were, the capital also had a seamy and unhygienic underside. Most citizens lived in multistory tenements the size of city blocks; these were known as *insulae* ("islands") because roads surrounded them. Only the very rich could afford the luxury of villas or of running water in their homes. Life in the *insulae* was crowded and unsanitary. Even though Rome had elaborate public sewers, they did not serve private buildings, and much household waste was simply dumped into the street. Fire was an additional hazard. The Great Fire of 64CE left only four of the capital's fourteen districts unscathed.

Yet for all its problems, the city remained a magnet throughout imperial times. Following Constantine's conversion to Christianity, the fourth century CE saw a new wave of construction, this time of churches. And even when the western Empire finally collapsed, Rome itself survived, buoyed by the prestige of its bishops, the popes. As the classical period gave way to the Middle Ages, the city remained an international capital, despite the fact that the source of its authority had moved from the political to the religious sphere.

RIGHT **Modern-day Rome, looking northeastward with the Palatine in the foreground and the Colosseum behind. Proverbially, Rome was not built in a day but grew steadily in size and splendor for more than a thousand years. Successive generations sought to embellish it further, often by knocking down what had been built before, so that few of the buildings of republican Rome eventually survived. The emperor Augustus, in particular, set out to reconstruct it on a grander scale, boasting toward the end of his life that he had found a city of brick and left a city of marble.**

THE ROMAN FORUM

Every Roman town, whatever its size, had a forum
where citizens could meet to gossip and do business.
Rome itself ended up with several forums bestowed
by rulers eager to leave their mark on the city.
Over the course of time, the forum of Julius Caesar
was followed by the forums of Augustus, Vespasian,
Nerva, and Trajan. But the oldest and most venerable
was always the Forum Romanum, or Roman Forum,
whose origins went back to the city's earliest days.

The space that the Roman Forum occupied started
life as a swampy valley in the shadow of the Capitoline
Hill. Archaeological investigation has shown that
it was used as a burial ground for cremation urns
as early as the tenth century BCE. By the late sixth
century, a formal square had been laid out.
Over succeeding centuries the Forum grew in
magnificence as fresh monuments were added.

Initially the Forum served as a marketplace as well
as a civic center, but in imperial times much of its
commercial activity passed to the newer, adjoining
centers. Yet the square continued to attract visitors
to the capital. They came to see the Tomb of Romulus,
the city's legendary founder, the Temple of Castor and
Pollux, divine patrons of the city, and the Rostra from
which generations of Roman orators had addressed
the people. Here, too, was the golden milestone from
which all distances in the Empire were measured,
for the Forum could truly claim to be the center
of the Roman world.

This atmospheric view of the Forum shows the Via
Sacra, which runs through the center of the complex.
In the middle is the small reconstructed Temple of
Vesta, with the Arch of Titus visible directly behind
in the distance. To the right are the three re-erected
columns of the Temple of Castor and Pollux.

PATRICIANS AND PLEBEIANS

The internal politics of early republican Rome were marked by a sharp class divide. On the one side were the patricians, the city's hereditary aristocracy; on the other, the plebeians, a heterogenous collection of people, ranging from jobless laborers and debt-ridden peasants to wealthy but non-noble landowners jealous of the patricians' grip on power. Just as the struggle for Italy dominated the first two centuries of the Republic's history, so the main theme of the internal politics of the period was the struggle between the two orders.

The origin of patrician power stretched back into the mists of time. As the historian Livy told the story, Romulus created 100 senators, known as "fathers," to help him govern early Rome, and the patricians were their descendants. Early on they established exclusive rights to the chief priestly offices, and they alone were able to take the auspices, which had to be consulted before major decisions were made. They also dominated the Senate.

Even though the patricians were a privileged oligarchy, many were highly public-spirited. Their code of civic duty was summed up in the career of L. Caecilius Metellus, who twice served as consul and saw distinguished service in the First Punic War. At his funeral in 221 BCE, his son insisted that he had achieved the most noble ambitions a Roman could hope for: "He was a warrior of the first rank, an excellent orator, and a courageous general; under his auspices, deeds of the greatest importance were accomplished; he attained the highest offices in the state; he was distinguished for his wisdom; he held primacy in the Senate; he won a large fortune by

BELOW **An early 4th-century CE mosaic from the Villa Romana del Casale in Sicily that depicts the unknown owner with his staff. Sicily's hinterland was divided into huge agricultural estates called** *latifundia*—**and the luxury of this villa suggests a property that belonged to a member of the uppermost social class.**

honorable means; he left behind many children; and he was the most famous man in the commonwealth."

The patrician families were linked to certain sections of the plebeians by a complex web of patronage and favors known as *clientela*—clienthood. However, there were also divisions between the orders that were based on classic class-struggle lines. A particular bone of contention was the patrician families' appropriation of public land for their own uses, and the economic burdens that led many small landholders to fall into a form of debt bondage known as *nexum*. Add in the thwarted political ambitions of Rome's incipient middle class, and the scene was set for a prolonged conflict that the plebeians eventually won.

The first plebeian consuls were elected in 366BCE, and soon the Senate started to fill up with "new men," as senators of non-noble birth were called. From 287BCE, the decisions of the plebeian Popular Assembly were given the full force of law. Yet the patricians continued to occupy a central position in the state. They played the part of successful ruling classes through the ages, compromising their exclusivity just enough to co-opt their most ambitious rivals into their own ranks, thereby averting the risk of revolution.

RIGHT **A bronze relief, 50–75CE, depicting two men, an older and a younger one, of a generic type—solemn-faced magistrates clad in togas and shoes appropriate to members of the patrician class. Even after the plebeians had achieved their political ambitions by gaining access to the Senate, the patricians continued to dominate the very highest public offices.**

PORTRAITS FOR POSTERITY

Carved cameos (left and right) were a common form of Roman portraiture, but
some of the most distinctive human likenesses came not from Rome itself but from
Egypt, which became part of the Roman Empire in 30BCE. These were the funerary
paintings known as Faiyum portraits, so-called because many of them came from
the Faiyum oasis (above, ca. 220–250CE; right, ca. 100–110CE). Painted on wood or
linen, the works, which faithfully depicted the appearance of the dead person,
were attached to the coffin before burial. The subjects were typically shown
gazing out unflinchingly, as though unafraid of death.

SLAVES AND FREEDMEN

For much of its history, Rome was a slave society on a massive scale, and servitude did much to corrupt and coarsen Roman life. Although the institution went back to early times, only the very rich could afford to keep slaves in the first centuries of the Republic. Everything changed with the wars of conquest of the second century BCE, after which hundreds of thousands of foreign captives were sold into slavery in Italy, 150,000 alone after Rome's victory against the Macedonians at Pydna in 168BCE. To compound the problem, pirates based on Crete and the Turkish coast roamed the eastern Mediterranean snatching victims for the slave market on the Aegean island of Delos, which was said to be able to handle 10,000 transactions a day. Many of these unfortunates also found their way to Italy.

The treatment they met there depended on fate and the disposition of their master. Many ended up working for the state, either as laborers or miners or, if they had an education, as clerks. Some had the good fortune to find themselves in

RIGHT **Detail from a 2nd-century CE North African mosaic depicting a slave hut and part of a fortified estate. Slaves provided a cheap source of labor for the big agricultural estates known as *latifundia*. Despite their desperate situation, they were permitted to own possessions, and some even amassed respectable sums of money from cash given to them by their owners.**

enlightened households where they were treated with humanity and warmth. The obverse, however, could be terrible: they could be tortured to extract confessions if a crime was committed, and, if a master was killed, every slave in the household was executed as a possible accomplice in the deed. Until the first century CE, masters could have male slaves castrated or sell them to die in the arena.

In general, the slaves' lot improved with time. Once the mass deportations of the last two centuries BCE came to an end, the price of slaves soared and the value put upon them rose with it. A master could give a slave his liberty at any time by performing a simple ceremony—these slaves became freedmen. They would then take the last name of their former master, and they and their immediate heirs continued to be bound to him by some residual ties of duty and obligation; two generations had to pass before their descendants became full Roman citizens. Even so, the descendants of slaves eventually became wholly integrated into the citizen body.

LEFT In this Roman bas-relief from the 2nd century CE, a slave is shown working in a kitchen. A study of Roman family names has revealed that, by late imperial times, eight out of ten Roman citizens had slave ancestry somewhere in their lineage.

SENATORS, CONSULS, AND TRIBUNES

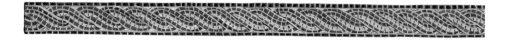

The constitution that Rome inherited from the Struggle of the Orders, pitting patricians against plebeians, was one of intricate checks and balances. The task of putting forward legislation lay with the Senate, which met in the Curia (Senate House) in the Roman Forum, or else in some other specially consecrated building in the capital. In the early days, there were 300 senators, chosen by the consuls from patrician ranks. Later the number expanded to 900 under Julius Caesar, although Augustus then reduced it to 600, and it became customary for ex-magistrates to be chosen, whether patrician or plebeian.

Besides proposing new laws, senators had other fingers on the strings of power. They controlled foreign policy, assigned magistrates to govern the provinces, and supervised the rituals of the state religion. They could also set up courts of enquiry to investigate wrongdoing. Through much of the Republic's life, they kept the executive under close supervision—indeed, when they finally lost control, the Republic collapsed and Rome was plunged into civil war. Senators gave up sovereign power under the Empire, although they continued to play an important role, supervising public finances and controlling some provinces.

The chief executive arms of government under the Republic were the two consuls, who had equal power. They were chosen by the *comitia centuriata*, a popular assembly, from the ranks of the senators, and the choice was ratified by the Senate. They held office for only a year, although they could be re-elected. Crucially, they commanded Rome's armies, often serving as generals in the field; in later times, they sometimes had their command extended so that they could serve as proconsuls governing conquered provinces. At home, they were assisted in the task of governing by such other magistrates as the *praetores*, who administered the

LEFT A *bisellium*, or consular chair, incorporated into the funerary stone of one Otacillius Oppianus, perhaps as the symbol of his office. The right to use a seat of this kind on public occasions was granted by local magistrates to honor distinguished persons.

law, the *aediles* in charge of public works, and the *quaestores* who oversaw state finances.

The tribunes of the people owed their existence to the Struggle of the Orders, when the office was created to represent plebeian interests against the patricians. Tribunes had themselves to be plebeians of free birth, and they were elected annually by the popular assembly. Their powers were considerable, for they could veto any act of any magistrate, and were protected from reprisal by their inviolate status—to harm a tribune merited the death penalty. The tribunes maintained their influence throughout the later centuries of the Republic only to lose it under the emperors, who assumed their powers for themselves, claiming to represent the people's interests in their own person.

ABOVE **A magistrate, seated in the center, is shown traveling in a procession, in this 2nd-century** BCE **Roman stone relief from Aquileia, Italy.**

FIRST AMONG EQUALS:
THE EMPEROR

For the greatest empire the Western world had known, the Roman *imperium* had inauspicious origins. Its founder, Octavian, deliberately avoided the title *imperator* (emperor), which was not used for the first fifty years of the Empire's existence. Instead, he chose to be known as *princeps*, a title implying "chief" or "first citizen," and to preserve the Senate and all the magistracies associated with republican government.

The reasons for Octavian's reticence were not hard to find. He was only too aware of the fate of his adoptive father Julius Caesar, who had been assassinated by men who feared his ambitions. To avoid Caesar's fate, he took care to downplay his intentions. He disbanded much of his army and continued to offer himself annually for re-election to the position of consul, which he had first held in the closing years of the war. The Senate responded gratefully by conferring on him the honorary name of Augustus ("revered one"). He was also given control over the army and assumed the post of tribune of the people, in effect using the mechanisms of republican government to attain absolute power.

Augustus always showed moderation in the use of his considerable powers, but the realities of absolute rule quickly made themselves felt under his successors. His immediate heir Tiberius had been a highly successful general, but he was an embittered and suspicious man when he eventually became emperor at the age of fifty-six, and his period in office deteriorated into a reign of terror. Caligula, his successor, proved even worse: under his erratic rule, autocracy tottered on the verge of

BELOW A sardonyx cameo, 1st century CE, bearing the profiles of two Roman emperors and their wives: Claudius and his wife Agrippina the Younger (left) and Germanicus and his wife Agrippina the Elder (right).

RIGHT Calm, youthful, dignified, but indisputably in command—a statue of the emperor Augustus. Known as *The Augustus of Prima Porta*, the statue was commissioned around 15 CE by his adopted son Tiberius and stood in the villa of Augustus's wife Livia at Prima Porta, outside Rome. According to the historian Suetonius, the emperor lived modestly by later imperial standards, wearing homespun cloth and using the same bed for 40 years.

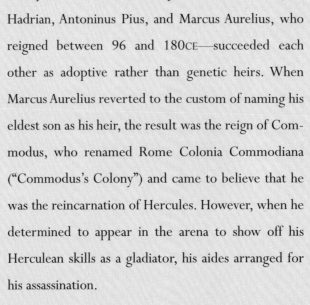

insanity. On one occasion, having determined to invade Britain, he lined his army up on Gaul's Channel shore only to set them to gathering seashells, which he described as "tribute from the Ocean." He then returned to Rome.

There would be other emperors scarcely better than Caligula in the Empire's long history—among them Nero, Domitian, and Elegabalus—although it is only fair to add that they were very much in a minority; the majority of rulers were conscientious and hard-working. A common feature linking most of the really incompetent emperors was the hereditary principle, which sometimes raised totally unsuitable candidates simply through accidents of birth. Significantly, the sequence of efficient rulers known to history as the "Five Good Emperors"—Nerva, Trajan, Hadrian, Antoninus Pius, and Marcus Aurelius, who reigned between 96 and 180CE—succeeded each other as adoptive rather than genetic heirs. When Marcus Aurelius reverted to the custom of naming his eldest son as his heir, the result was the reign of Commodus, who renamed Rome Colonia Commodiana ("Commodus's Colony") and came to believe that he was the reincarnation of Hercules. However, when he determined to appear in the arena to show off his Herculean skills as a gladiator, his aides arranged for his assassination.

From the third century on, the emperors spent less and less time in Rome as the threat to the Empire's frontiers grew. Now a new danger arose as the rulers became increasingly beholden to the army. Emperors were made and unmade by the legions with

LEFT **This early 4th-century CE sculpture, once found in Constantinople but now embedded into the corner of the façade of the Basilica San Marco, Venice, shows the emperor Diocletian with his co-regents Maximian, Galerius, and Constantius, collectively known as the tetrarchy. Their standardized forms and features indicate their equality; their embraces symbolize unity. Under Diocletian, each co-regent oversaw a different part of the Empire. One had his capital in Trier in Germany, another in Milan, a third in Thessalonica, while Diocletian himself chose to rule from Nicomedia (modern-day Izmit, Turkey).**

dizzying rapidity: thirty-one individuals aspired to the title in the fifty years after 235CE, sometimes more than one at a time. Diocletian restored some order in the late third century, but only by recognizing that the task of holding the Empire together was more than one man could handle. Instead he established the tetrarchy, a power-sharing arrangement that divided the imperial duties between four co-regents, each supervising different regions. This step paved the way for the division of the Empire into eastern and western components. Rome itself ceased even to be an imperial headquarters, although it remained the seat of the Senate.

Diocletian also finally abandoned any remaining notion of simply being first among equals of the Roman people. Instead, he chose to rule in oriental splendor, endorsing a tendency that had already been visible in some of his immediate prede-cessors. Although he elected not to identify himself as a god, he and his fellow emperors were regularly portrayed as companions of gods, Hercules and Jupiter being the preferred models. Ironically, Diocletian chose at the same time to encour-age a cult of Rome and the Roman people, even though the city itself was gradually moving to the sidelines of history.

There were great rulers in the last centuries of Roman power who managed to unify the Empire under their personal rule; Constantine, who defeated all his rivals to rule single-handedly between 324 and 337CE, was probably the greatest. Yet the world had changed in the intervening years, and Constantine's rule was very differ-ent from the consensual mock-republicanism of Augustus's day. Constantine himself recognized the shifting balance of power by building the great new imperial capital of Constantinople near the Empire's eastern borders. It was a far-sighted move, for the future was to lie with the Greek-speaking Byzantine world ruled from that city, whose emperors would cling onto power for almost a thousand years after Rome itself had fallen and power in the west had passed to the barbarians.

EMBLEMS OF POWER

The exercise of power was imperial Rome's central concern, and symbols of authority played a vital part in its official iconography. The eagle was associated not just with speed and strength but also with the sky and the sun. The Romans linked the bird to their own supreme sky god, Jupiter—the eagle then became the bird of the emperors, Jupiter's earthly equivalents, and also transferred naturally to emblematic military use, such as legion standards (left and right). The imposing, and rare, statue of an eagle (opposite) is in bronze, ca. 100–300CE. Another popular iconographic form of image-building was the use of cameos to profile gods and goddesses, heroes and rulers—the example here (above) bears the head of Tiberius (reigned 14–37CE).

CONQUEST AND GLORY

No Roman institution could match the army for prestige. The nation owed its success to its martial prowess, which had turned a small Italian city-state into a world power. Unsurprisingly, then, the military virtues of discipline, order, duty, and loyalty were central to the Roman ethos.

For most of its early history, however, Rome made do without professional soldiers. The republican forces that conquered peninsular Italy in the fifth and fourth centuries BCE consisted of ad-hoc levies drawn from the ranks of male, property-owning citizens between the ages of seventeen and forty-six. The majority of recruits were peasant farmers, summoned to Rome when they were needed. They were expected to provide their own weapons and equipment and were at first unremunerated for their efforts, although pay was eventually introduced as campaigns grew longer.

Even so, the levy system eventually broke down as Rome's military commitments widened. Volunteers called upon to serve in the ranks for months or even years at a time could not combine their obligations with the demands of running a farm or advancing a career. So the consul Gaius Marius introduced a radical reform program at the end of the first century BCE. He abandoned conscription and the property requirement, and instead enlisted volunteers who agreed to sign up for a sixteen-year term. He also improved the equipment and weaponry of the legions, which were now provided entirely by the state.

In effect, Marius created a professional standing army—one that proved a formidably effective fighting force. However, the weakness of the Marian system was that the full-time soldiers relied on military success for their advancement, and increasingly their loyalties were given not to the state as a whole but rather to individual commanders. An ambitious general like Julius Caesar could gain the devotion of his men not just by winning battles but also by rewarding them fittingly (he almost doubled their pay). The ultimate loser was Rome itself, which was plunged into the horrors of the civil war.

When Augustus restored peace and order from 29BCE on, he reduced the number of legions from about sixty to twenty-eight and paid off the redundant soldiery generously with grants of money and land. The new military structure he went on to create formed the basis for Roman might throughout the imperial period.

Each legion of the Roman army was divided into cohorts and centuries. These last were usually made up of about eighty men under the command of a centurion.

BELOW A spectacular view of a section of Hadrian's Wall, near Housesteads, Northumberland, England, in winter. The emperor Hadrian built the wall in the early 2nd century CE to separate Roman Britain from the unconquered lands to the north. The wall still stands, at least in part, stretching for some 73 miles (117km) from the River Tyne to the Solway Firth.

Total numbers varied, but in early imperial times typically averaged about 5,500 men. In battle, the legions traditionally formed up in three lines: the *hastati* or spearmen at the forefront, with the *principes* ("men in their prime") behind them, and a reserve of veterans, the *triarii* (third-rankers), taking up the rear.

The legions were supplemented by auxiliary forces composed of volunteers from outside Italy, serving under Roman commanders. They were paid much less than legionaries and had to serve for twenty-five years. However, they became eligible on retirement for Roman citizenship, which they could pass on to their heirs.

The Roman navy never commanded the esteem afforded to the army. Indeed, for the first two centuries of the Republic, there was no navy at all. Rome only felt the need for a maritime force when its ambitions spread beyond Italy itself, at the time of the First Punic War in the mid-third century BCE. The Senate then ordered a fleet to be created out of nothing: the call was for 100 *quinqueremes*—long warships with five banks of oars—to be built in just sixty days. The hastily assembled armada acquitted itself surprisingly well against the master mariners of Carthage, partly due to the fact that the Romans adapted existing ship designs so that they could fight on their own terms.

Under the emperors the navy guaranteed freedom of trade and ensured that the Mediterranean remained what the Romans called *Mare Nostrum*—"our sea." The principal naval base was at Misenum, near Naples, but there was also a naval presence on the outer fringes of the Empire. A river fleet guarded the Rhine, while a squadron stationed at Boulogne patrolled the Channel and even once circumnavigated Britain, discovering the Orkney Islands. Sailors were referred to as *milites* (soldiers) like their counterparts on land, and were commanded in the same fashion as legionaries. Even so, most were non-Italians. The Roman genius was for land warfare, and it was by infantrymen that the Empire was won and primarily maintained.

PHILOSOPHERS AND POETS

Although Rome's early citizens showed a deep suspicion of philosophy, the discipline soon established a grip on the imagination of at least a cultivated minority of the population. Roman tastes never ran much toward abstract speculation; on the whole, interest focused on ethical questions. One exception was the poet Lucretius, whose epic *De Rerum Natura* ("On the Nature of Things") was a passionate, versified exposition of the materialist worldview of the Greek philosopher Epicurus, an early exponent of the atomic theory of matter.

For the most part, though, Roman thinkers inclined more to Stoicism than to Epicureanism, finding practical solace in the Stoic ideal of philosophical detachment from life's tribulations. One of the most eloquent exponents of this view was the emperor Marcus Aurelius (ca. 161–180CE), who jotted down his *Meditations* in moments snatched from campaigning against barbarians on the Empire's frontiers.

Latin literature similarly derived from Greek roots, and wealthy *culturati* like Cicero chose to send their children to be educated in Athens. Yet it quickly developed a genius of its own, attracting an enthusiastic audience boosted by the spread of literacy through large sections of the population. There was also an audience for public recitations. Even so, apart from Virgil (see pages 90–93), most poets struggled to find an audience or to make a living. Manuscripts had to be copied lengthily by hand onto papyrus rolls, and the publishers who employed the copyists paid no royalties. As a result, literature remained mainly a pursuit of the leisured classes, except for a few fortunate talents who attracted the support of wealthy patrons.

RIGHT The Greek philosopher Plato (third from the left) conversing with other philosophers in the Academy (1st-century CE mosaic, from Pompeii). Both Roman philosophy and literature were deeply rooted in the intellectual traditions of the Greeks— so much so that the Roman poet Horace's advice to the young was, "Read the Greeks by night and read the Greeks by day."

LEFT A group of philosophers is depicted in high relief on a late 3rd-century CE Roman sarcophagus from Acilia. Early Romans were suspicious of philosophy— when the first Greek teachers reached Rome in the second century BCE, they were expelled. And in 161BCE, according to the historian Suetonius, "it was decreed, following discussions in the Senate, that philosophers and rhetoricians should not be allowed to live in Rome."

ROMANS AND BARBARIANS

Sociologists in many parts of the world trace the origins of nationalism and racism to our primitive urge to divide the outside world into "us" and "them." Few cultures have articulated the division as succinctly as the Romans, who used the term "barbarian" to describe whatever was alien to their own classical worldview.

The word came originally from the Greek—Homer coined it to describe the yawping speech patterns of the Carians of Asia Minor, which sounded discordant to Hellenic ears. It subsequently developed into a pejorative term used to indicate anything foreign and undesirable; as such, it was applied with particular vehemence to the Persian invaders of the fifth century BCE. Ironically, the Romans, who later appropriated the term,

RIGHT A detail from Trajan's Column—the memorial column erected in Rome to celebrate the emperor's successful campaigns in Dacia, north of the Danube River, in what is now Romania. The scene shows Trajan sacrificing a bull to Neptune before embarking on a second campaign in 105–106CE, after the Dacian king Decebalus had broken the peace terms of the first war (101–102CE).

were themselves typical barbarians to Greek eyes—a people of inferior culture excelling only in force of arms.

After Rome's conquest of Greece in the second century BCE, the concept of barbarism as an antonym for civilization was absorbed by the conquerors along with many other aspects of Hellenistic culture. The Romans were selective in their use of the term, applying it not to all foreigners but only to those who fell beyond the confines of the classical heritage. Romans were often scathing about the Greek people, many of whom they enslaved. They called them weak, effeminate, cowardly, and corrupt—but they never accused them of being barbarians.

The Roman use of the word was by no means arbitrary, for the culture gap that it addressed was a very real one. Roman (and Greek) society was urban and economically developed—different in every way from the tribal agricultural societies that the Romans confronted beyond their borders, at least in Europe and North Africa. Although the barbarian lands had a rich imaginative life, expressed in myth and folktale, and sometimes produced fine artworks, they had no equivalent of the high culture of Rome's educated classes, and for the most part lacked writing.

In time, familiarity led certain barbarian elites to admire and even embrace aspects of Roman culture, just as the conquered peoples of the Empire did. Yet those barbarians who found their way to Rome only to die in the arenas or to be worked to death as slaves in mines or on the great agricultural estates can hardly have formed any very high opinion of the general superiority of Roman civilization.

In the long run, the chasm that divided the Roman and barbarian worlds was to prove fatal to the western Empire. In the east, Romans shared many common values with their subject peoples, who became integrated in a way that the inhabitants of the western lands failed to do. Although Roman culture radically altered Gaul and Spain and North Africa and Britain, it remained, in comparison, a surface veneer that rubbed off easily under the pressure of the great invasions of the fifth century. The barbarians took their revenge when the legions finally withdrew.

BATTLES COMMEMORATED

Powerful Romans cherished their reputations in death as they did in life. While emperors sought to prolong their fame by building great monuments, other leading citizens made do by spending considerable sums on their tombs. From about 100CE on, when burial replaced cremation as the usual funerary arrangement, decorated sarcophagi—stone coffins— became an important medium for sculptors, who found a reliable market for their work among patrons seeking lasting memorials.

Specialist workshops were soon established in Rome, Athens, and other centers to meet the demand. To judge by evidence from shipwrecks, works from provincial studios were sometimes shipped half-finished to Italy, where a local artist would add a portrait of the deceased to round them off. Mythology provided favorite scenes for the side-panels, along with Dionysiac revels or vignettes of the seasons or marine life.

Battle scenes also became popular from the mid-2nd century on—a time when barbarian forces were pressing with increasing urgency on the Empire's frontiers. One of the finest examples is the Ludovisi sarcophagus (ca. 251CE; see illustration, right), now preserved in Rome's Palazzo Altemps, part of the Museo Nazionale Romano. Typically, its teeming reliefs show clean-shaven legionaries in battle with bearded Germans. Historians have suggested that the central figure, shown on horseback and serene amid the mayhem, may be Hostilian (d. 251CE), the younger son of the emperor Decius (ruled 249–251CE). Ironically, while Decius and his eldest son Etruscus died in battle against the Goths, Hostilian himself spent his short life in Rome, where he fell victim to the plague shortly after his father's demise.

A CITIZEN'S LIFE

LEFT A highly idealized vision of life in ancient Rome is presented in this 4th-century CE mosaic depicting a river landscape with a magnificent villa in the foreground. For a majority of both the rural and the urban population, however, life would have appeared very different. At the bottom end of the social scale, for example, slave laborers were often confined to bolted and barred dormitories that were little better than prisons; household servants may have enjoyed greater comfort and were sometimes given a small bedroom of their own.

Wealthy Romans had little doubt that they lived in the greatest city the world had ever seen, and their provincial counterparts also had few reasons to complain. In the Empire's prosperous days, Roman citizens enjoyed a standard of living that was almost certainly the highest yet known. However, these fortunates formed only a small minority of the total population. Most people lived in servants' quarters or army barracks, in crowded, noisy tenements or malodorous rural hovels. Daily life in the Empire covered a wide spectrum of lifestyles in which one person's creature comforts were often earned by the sweat of another's brow, and where luxury and squalor coexisted in close proximity.

BELOW The ancient Romans often placed curses on their enemies in texts inscribed in lead—these are known as curse tablets. In this example, doubtless written by a jilted lover or husband, the embittered text includes the passage: "May he who carried Sylvia off from me become as liquid as water." (Romano-British, 2nd to 4th century CE.)

CHILDHOOD AND SCHOOLING

In early republican times, the education of Roman children was left very much in the hands of parents. Cato the Elder, in the second century BCE, refused to entrust his son's upbringing to an educated Greek slave living in his own household. Instead, Plutarch tells us, Cato himself "taught his son reading and writing, the law, physical education, and all sorts of outdoor skills such as throwing the javelin, fighting in armor, riding, boxing, swimming, and how to stand up to heat and cold." Such a man would also expect his boy to follow him in the course of his public duties, whether to the temple for religious observances or to social events, including dinner parties—even to the Senate, if his father were a member.

Later Romans, however, increasingly entrusted their children to teachers, although there was never anything resembling a state school system. Wealthy families might employ a slave, like Cato's educated Greek, to act as a private tutor. Less well-off parents sent their children from about the age of seven, whether boys or girls, to a schoolmaster to learn reading, writing, and arithmetic. These poorly paid individuals held classes in their own homes, or sometimes in rented stalls in the streets. Discipline was harsh, administered with the cane or leather belt. Children learned to write using bone or metal styluses on wax tablets, which could be wiped clean and reused—papyrus rolls were too expensive for school exercises.

Primary schooling came to an end at about age eleven. Following this, the majority of girls were educated at home, learning how to run a household—cooking, spinning, weaving, fetching water, or, if the parents were well-off, giving orders to slaves. Boys, however, might pass on into the hands of a *grammaticus*, Rome's equivalent of a high school teacher, to study Greek and Roman literature. The more

ABOVE Some ancient Roman toys were similar to those played with by young children today, including rattles, dolls, and animals in various different forms, such as this wooden mouse with a moving jaw. For the majority of children between the ages of 7 and 11, schooling started soon after dawn and continued until early afternoon—after this, they were free to go to the baths or else home to play with friends.

RIGHT A 1st-century CE wall painting from Herculaneum depicts a young woman, watched over by her mother, as she learns to play the cithara, an ancient string instrument resembling the harp.

ambitious students might then go on to a rhetorician for lessons in oratory in preparation for a career in public life or the law.

Of the two languages of learning, Greek carried the greater prestige, and some fortunate students went to Greece to complete their education. For poorer parents, the choices were much more stark, even to the point of infanticide. A letter sent to his pregnant wife by a legionary serving in Egypt acts as a reminder of the realities of parenthood for much of the population: "If you give birth to a boy, keep it. If it is a girl, expose it. Try not to worry. I'll send the money as soon as we get paid."

THE ROMAN HOME

The homes in which Romans lived varied greatly according to each individual's wealth and status. At the top of the social pyramid, the wealthy luxuriated in marble villas, their walls bright with frescoes and their floors rich in mosaics. Very affluent individuals might have two or more such residences, one in town and the other in the country, often at the heart of a vast agricultural estate.

By the imperial era, the prosperous middle classes could also aspire to comfortable villas. The general plan was one of rooms leading on to an atrium with an open skylight that let in both sunlight and rain (collected in a small pool called the *impluvium*). This provided both a large, central public space and opportunities for privacy. The bigger villas also had a second courtyard, the *peristylum*, which was colonnaded, following the Greek fashion, and often served as a garden. Further sophistications, including central heating, followed in imperial times. Glass sometimes came to supplement wooden shutters in windows, although it remained thick and opaque.

Most inhabitants of Rome itself enjoyed few luxuries. The mass of the population lived in crowded, rank tenements that were up to five or six stories high—the emperor Augustus limited their height to reduce the ever-present risk of fire. Although there were owner-occupiers, the majority of people rented rooms from wealthy landlords or speculative builders—prices in Rome were about four times higher than those found elsewhere in Italy.

Noise pollution was a major problem for city-dwellers. The poet Martial, who lived in a third-floor apartment, complained that, "There's no peace and quiet in the city for a poor man. Early in the morning, schoolmasters stop us enjoying any normal life. Before it gets light there are the bakers, then it's the hammering of the coppersmiths all day." Nights were little better because the use of heavy transport was restricted to after dark to relieve congestion in the daylight hours.

For all the complaints, city apartments were in constant demand; even Martial found that he grew homesick for the bustle of Rome when he retired to a Spanish villa. Tenement living was made bearable by the fact that much of the day was spent out of the house: in the streets, at the circus, and, above all, at the public baths.

LEFT View of the Casa del Fauno ("House of the Faun"), Pompeii, Italy, named after the bronze statue of the dancing faun that graces its rainwater pool. This elegant patrician residence is the largest of its kind in Pompeii and extends over nearly 10,000 square feet (3,000 square meters). Four dining rooms, two spacious gardens, and a magnificent mosaic of the Battle of Issus (between Alexander the Great and Darius III, now in the Archaeological Museum in Naples) were among the villa's many notable features.

ABOVE A communal lavatory (Roman, ca. 127CE), part of the Hadrianic bath complex at Leptis Magna, North Africa. Public baths made a significant contribution to the health and well-being of the inhabitants of the cities during the imperial era, providing many of the facilities for exercise and hygiene that were lacking in the majority of urban homes.

THE ART OF MOSAIC

The Romans quickly developed a taste for mosaics, which reached Rome from Greece in the second century BCE. Workshops sprang up in many parts of the Empire to cater to the market. The tiny stone *tesserae* used to compose the designs were mostly cut by slaves—as many as 1.5 million might be needed to lay a floor just 49 square feet (15 square meters). The Roman mosaics illustrated here show: (opposite) a child riding a dolphin and chasing a sea monster, from the House of Bacchus, Cuicil (modern Djemila, Algeria), 1st century CE; and (above) a head of Autumn from Corinium (modern Cirencester, England), 2nd century CE.

FEATS OF ENGINEERING

Among the ancient Romans' most impressive achievements was the development of highly sophisticated engineering techniques that enabled fresh water supplies to be carried into the cities. Although only the very wealthy could afford running water in their own homes—most citizens had to fetch their supply from the nearest fountain or buy it from a water carrier—the new feats of engineering nevertheless transformed people's daily lives, contributing greatly to their health and comfort.

Through their mastery of the arch as a structural component, engineers and architects were able to combine science and artistry to construct huge monuments such as the magnificent aqueduct Pont du Gard (right) in what is now France, erected ca. 19BCE to carry water and traffic over the Gard River to Nîmes, 16 miles (26km) away. The upper span of thirty-five small arches is about 900 feet (275m) long and 10 feet (3m) wide; it supported a conduit that carried fresh water 161 feet (49m) above the river. The lowest span runs for about half this length and is approximately 39 feet (12m) wide. Constructed of stone blocks entirely without mortar, the aqueduct formed part of a skilfully engineered system of water channels that ran in all for some 31 miles (50km). Much of its course can still be traced today.

Of equal sophistication was the engineering infrastructure of the city of Rome itself. By late imperial times, eleven aqueducts, covering a total of 270 miles (435km), brought millions of gallons of water into the city each day. The water fed into distribution tanks, from which it was carried in lead pipes to public fountains and baths.

THE DOMESTIC WORLD

"There is nothing more holy, nothing more securely guarded by every religious instinct, than each individual Roman's home," Cicero claimed. And the chief responsibility for preserving its sanctity rested squarely on the shoulders of the *paterfamilias,* or father of the family, who had powers, in theory at least, of life and death over his children. Not only could he order them to be exposed at birth, leaving them to die, he could also hand them over to execution or into slavery, if he so chose—although, needless to say, such behavior was extremely rare.

Wives were expected to conduct themselves with dignity and circumspection. Often they married at fourteen or fifteen, at which tender age they were already expected to take charge of the day-to-day running of the household. In even moderately wealthy families, that meant directing the work of domestic slaves. Well-to-do women left the nursing, and sometimes the upbringing of infants, to servants.

State policy generally favored large families, and—officially, at least—adultery and extramarital affairs were regarded with horror. In 18BCE, Augustus passed a law that allowed a father to kill his daughter and her lover with impunity if they were caught *in flagrante* ("in the act"), and that similarly permitted a husband to kill an adulterous rival, although not his wife; instead, he was expected to divorce her promptly or face punishment. Such a woman could not remarry and lost a third of her property; she also faced banishment to an island. The adulterer, if not killed on the spot, lost half his property and could also expect to be deported to an island, although not the same one as the adultress. Such strictures were no doubt aimed primarily at Rome's fast set, a particular cause of concern to the reforming emperor. A more typical picture of Roman family life comes from tombstones, which sometimes bear touching messages of marital affection that echo down the centuries.

RIGHT In ancient Rome, as throughout the modern world, dogs were not only kept as domestic pets but were also often used as guards and protectors to deter thieves or unwanted visitors from private property. The dog on a leash shown here is an example of a late 1st-century CE *cave canum* ("beware of the dog") mosaic from Pompeii.

ROMAN WOMEN

There was a marked tension between what Roman men expected a woman's role to be and women's own view of the subject, at least among the affluent classes. The traditional and officially accepted male view was of women as home-makers. *Lanam fecit*—"she made wool"—was a eulogy frequently incised on women's tombstones. The emperor Augustus himself insisted on wearing only clothes made from homespun wool, although, needless to say, the actual weaving in the imperial household was done by domestic slaves.

RIGHT Detail from a 1st-century CE fresco from Herculaneum depicting a young slave woman combing the hair of a girl while two other women look on. Perhaps the most fortunate of slave women were those who became domestic servants in prosperous households, where they could usually expect reasonable treatment. Even so, the satirist Juvenal speaks of bad-tempered mistresses slapping and pulling the hair of clumsy servants if their coiffure was not arranged correctly.

Legally, the position of women was
not strong. Daughters were almost entirely in
their fathers' power. In early times, husbands exercised similar authority over their wives after marriage,
but the wives' rights increased with time, and, by the late
republican period, they could for the most part retain control of their own property, even though their financial
affairs had to be handled by a male guardian. But
women in Rome certainly had greater liberty
to get out of the house than their counterparts in ancient Greece and could, for example,
go shopping or attend the theater on their own.

For some high-born women, emancipation
went well beyond such modest bounds. One such was Clodia, who has gone down
in literary history as the "Lesbia" of Catullus's impassioned love poems. Catullus
was, however, very far from being her only lover. The wife of a consul and a member of the high-ranking Claudian family, she became the central figure in a trial that
scandalized Rome in 57BCE. She was the accuser, charging a former lover with brib-
ing slaves to poison her. The accused was fortunate to have Cicero, an old acquain-
tance, as his advocate. He succeeded in getting the young man acquitted.

The most unfortunate of Roman women were the slaves, although some fared
better than others. One serious problem was that slave girls were regarded as the
property of their masters, and so had no legal recourse in cases of sexual harrass-
ment or rape. Even so, their fate was possibly preferable to that of the slaves condemned to a life of drudgery in the inns and taverns. A law of the early fourth
century spelled out that they could not be accused of adultery because it was taken
for granted that they would have sexual relations with the male clientele. Their
rights were, quite simply, beneath the law's cognizance.

FOOD AND DRINK

Most Romans lived quite frugally. They ate breakfasts consisting of little more than bread and fruit, perhaps with olives and honey. By imperial times it was normal to have a light lunch (*prandium*) shortly before noon. The main meal (*cena*) was taken around sunset, when the day's work was finished.

The poor lived mainly on a porridge of ground wheat mixed with water, known as *puls*; this staple could be made tastier and more nutritious by the addition of cheese, honey, or an egg, if such ingredients were available. In republican days, the elder Cato, an economically minded employer, recommended feeding slaves on bread, windfall olives, oil, salt, cheap wine, and the dregs of fish sauce.

In Rome itself, the poorest free citizens could count on the corn dole to protect them from starvation. Initially introduced as a subsidized-food scheme by the consul Gaius Gracchus (ca. 160–121 BCE), this project was vastly extended at Julius

RIGHT **Color played an important part in Roman domestic interiors, mainly in the form of painted plaster or stucco. This still life with bowls of fruit and a wine jar is a fresco from the Casa di Julia Fericus ("House of Julia Felix"), Pompeii, 1st century BCE.**

Caesar's behest as a way of securing support and subsequently became a fixture of life in the capital. Under its terms, a given number of individuals (200,000 under Augustus, although the number varied over the centuries) received handouts of free wheat each month. The cost was borne by the state out of general taxation.

Those Romans who were eligible for the corn dole were happy to receive it, even if their needs were not great. In early imperial times, most citizens could in fact afford to eat well, and a wide range of produce was available. Fish was generally more plentiful than meat, although pork was a firm favorite. There was a good variety of poultry, game birds, and wildfowl. Shellfish were esteemed, including oysters raised in artificial beds. Many different types of bread were produced. Romans ate eggs and cheese in large quantities, but regarded butter as a food for barbarians; their principal fat was olive oil.

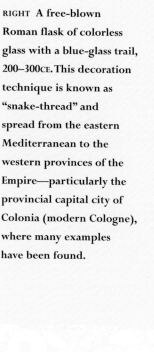

RIGHT A free-blown Roman flask of colorless glass with a blue-glass trail, 200–300CE. This decoration technique is known as "snake-thread" and spread from the eastern Mediterranean to the western provinces of the Empire—particularly the provincial capital city of Colonia (modern Cologne), where many examples have been found.

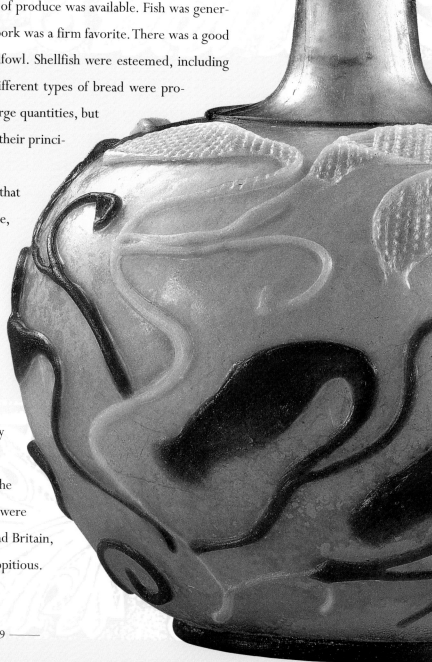

Apart from water, the only drink that was consumed in large amounts was wine, which was usually diluted with water. Archaeologists have noted that grape pips that have been discovered only appear in strata under the capital from the last quarter of the seventh century BCE on, so it is possible that the cultivation of vines was not native to Latium and was introduced, like so much else, by the Etruscans. Certainly, a taste for the grape subsequently spread throughout the Empire, and the only provinces that were without vineyards were northern Gaul and Britain, where the climate at the time was not propitious.

While the majority of Romans may have lived abstemiously, the new rich of imperial times became famous for their excesses. As the Empire grew wealthier, its people became greedier. In Nero's day, the philosopher Seneca accused his fellow-citizens of "eating till they vomited and of vomiting in order to eat more."

A taste for conspicuous consumption followed the increase in prosperity brought about by the spread of trade. Exotic delicacies became fashionable, and wealthy diners regaled themselves with specialities like roast peacock, mullets' livers, and flamingos' tongues. The gourmet Apicius, to whom the only surviving Roman cookbook is ascribed, provides a menu for boiled ostrich. "Bring pepper, mint, roasted cumin, parsleyseed, dates, honey, vinegar, cooking wine, fish stock, and a little oil to the boil in a saucepan. Thicken the sauce with cornflour. Pour over the pieces of ostrich meat in a serving dish and sprinkle with pepper."

The apotheosis of Roman nouveau-riche dining is Trimalchio's feast, as described in Petronius Arbiter's novel, the *Satyricon*. Petronius was a satirist and given to exaggeration, but even so, the banquet he described would not have raised a smile among his readers unless it had some grounding in reality. The highlight of the meal comes when a huge wild pig is brought into the banqueting room preceded by a pack of hunting dogs; its roasted skin conceals a flock of live thrushes. Other features of the meal include a hare dressed up with wings to resemble the flying horse Pegasus, a goose garnished with small birds sculpted from roast pork, and roast dormice dipped in honey and rolled in poppyseed.

Real life in fact presented fitting role models for satire. One L. Aelius Verus is said to have provided mules for his dinner guests to carry away the gifts of gold, silver, and crystalware that he offered. Yet for outrageous extravagance, no private citizens could rival the more decadent emperors. Vitellius—one of the short-lived rulers of the disastrous "Year of the Four Emperors" (see page 12)—went down in

RIGHT A maenad and two satyrs—the carousing attendants of Bacchus, god of wine—are shown in procession in this marble relief, 100CE, from the Villa Quintilli on the Appian Way. Ancient Rome's wine connoisseurs particularly appreciated the product of Falernian vineyards. There was even a legendary vintage, that of 121BCE, whose produce was treasured among the very wealthy well into imperial days. But most Romans never aspired to any such delights, although they may have enjoyed the odd tipple of *mulsum*—a sweet dessert wine produced by mixing grape must with honey.

history as "the Glutton." A banquet given for his arrival in Rome featured 2,000 fish and 7,000 game birds; he also concocted a dish whose ingredients—pike livers, peacock and pheasant brains, flamingo tongues, lamprey milt—had to be fetched by warships from all quarters of the Empire. Yet even his reputation was eclipsed by Elagabalus, a third-century emperor from Syria who allegedly hosted dinners featuring peas served with grains of gold; at one of them, so many rose petals were released from the ceiling that several guests suffocated. His rumored excesses did not go unpunished—he was assassinated within four years of claiming the throne.

THE WAREHOUSE OF THE WORLD

The Roman Empire, in its heyday, was a vast free-trade area encompassing the entire Mediterranean world. A single currency was in use from the Scottish border to Syria. The sea was plied by merchant ships carrying loads of up to 400 tons, while on land a first-class road system encouraged the exchange of goods within and between far-flung provinces. The trading momentum only faltered from the third century on, when a combination of high taxes and galloping inflation sapped prosperity, paving the way for the western Empire's eventual decline.

In its most affluent years, Rome itself was the focus of mercantile activity. "The warehouse of the world," a Greek visitor called it, adding that "whatever is raised or manufactured by every people is always here in superabundance." Goods flowed into Ostia and its near neighbor, the purpose-built harbor of Portus Augusti, for transport up the Tiber by barge to the city itself. The most vital supplies were the grain shipments that fed the city: 400,000 tons were imported annually, mainly from Egypt and Sicily.

The capital also had an insatiable appetite for luxury goods. Merchants imported silks from China by way of India, ivory from Africa, and furs from

LEFT A butcher at work (2nd-century CE relief). Advising his son on suitable professions for a gentleman, the politician and orator Cicero insisted that retail trade should be despised. "Least respectable of all," he suggested, "are the trades catering for sensual pleasures: fishmongers, butchers, cooks, poulterers, fishermen. You can add perfumers, dancers, and entertainers." The Roman elite may have enjoyed the produce of trade, but they did not deign to engage in it.

northern Europe. There was a particularly well-established trade in amber, which found its way from the Baltic region to the north Italian town of Aquileia, where it was transformed into jewelry and ornaments. Aromatic resins and spices—especially pepper—were in demand to satisfy the Roman taste for strongly flavored food, and the demand was met via long-distance trade routes stretching eventually to India and southeast Asia.

For all the excellence of the Roman roads, most goods traveled by boat; horse-drawn vehicles simply could not rival the carrying capacity of ships when it came to bulk transport. Yet seaborne trade itself carried risks that ruined many an entrepreneur, for the Mediterranean was liable to unpredictable storms, particularly between the months of November and March. However, the rewards more than justified the risks—many of the Empire's biggest fortunes were first made in shipping.

Goods reached the public through shops that might not seem wholly unfamiliar in Mediterranean cities to this day. The most obvious difference was the lack of shop windows; instead, premises opened directly onto the street, to be closed off at night by wooden shutters. Shopkeepers piled up their wares on the pavement outside, until the emperor Domitian passed an edict banning the practice. An important difference from modern times was that almost all of the shopkeepers were either slaves or freedmen. Freeborn Romans never overcame a repugnance for trade.

ABOVE A collection of 3rd-century CE Roman coins, part of a hoard from the Crimea, where Rome's currency was in common use for trade. Rome had made its presence felt on the edge of the steppes and in the Black Sea, or Pontus Euxinus, region in the 1st century CE, establishing protectorates and bases where legionaries were stationed in strategic locations.

RICHES OF THE NILE

Egyptian civilization intrigued the Romans just as it continues to beguile people around the world today. Travelers' tales of Egypt's ancient monuments and bizarre, animal-headed gods had gone the rounds of the classical world since at least Herodotus's day in the fifth century BCE. The scandalous activities of the last pharaoh, Queen Cleopatra, added to its allure—not only did she bear a son to Julius Caesar, but then, by her well-publicized affair with Mark Antony, also helped trigger the civil war that finally put an end to the Republic. Thereafter, Egypt became a province of the Roman Empire, and the rich harvests of the Black Lands regularly inundated by the Nile River provided Rome's most important source of grain, vital for feeding the capital's population, as well as exotic animals destined for the Colosseum.

Among the enduring products of the Roman fascination with things Egyptian are several large mosaics depicting fanciful scenes of life in the Nile Valley, such as the example shown here (right, mid-1st century BCE), which originally came from the vicinity of the temple of Fortuna at Praeneste (modern Palestrina, where it is now in the archaeological museum). There are other extant examples from Pompeii, Roman Galilee, and Asia Minor. The Praeneste mosaic shows the inundation of the Nile and the hunting of its bountiful animal life.

Constructed at the temple so that it was bathed by the waters of a fountain, the mosaic seems to have been produced by Alexandrian artists working sometime in the mid-first century BCE for a patron with a particular interest in Egypt—conceivably even Cleopatra herself, who visited Rome in 46 BCE. Despite the fact that they came from Egypt, their knowledge of the fauna was limited: although hippopotamuses and crocodiles are portrayed with reasonable accuracy, depictions of other animals are unconvincing.

TOWN AND COUNTRY

The Romans were urbanizers par excellence. Wherever they went they took the habits of city living with them, even to areas of the Empire such as northern Gaul and Britain where towns were novelties. The situation was different in the eastern provinces, which already had a long urban tradition. There, too, however, urban communities flourished as never before under the *Pax Romana*, reaching levels of prosperity unmatched in earlier times.

The new foundations tended to follow a fixed pattern. They were built to a grid plan and were surrounded by defensive walls penetrated by several guarded

RIGHT Detail from a 1st-century CE Pompeiian wall painting depicting a bird in a garden. In ancient Rome, as in the modern day, city life was stressful, and, in their private moments, Romans dreamed of country peace. Even Petronius, author of the highly urban *Satyricon*, shared the same idyll: "Small house and quiet roof tree, shadowing elm,/Grapes on the vine and cherries ripening,/ Red apples in the orchard, Pallas' tree/Breaking with olives, and well-watered earth,/And fields of kale and heavy creeping mallows/And poppies that will surely bring me sleep."

LEFT The residential quarter of a Roman walled town is shown in this stone relief (Claudian era, 41–54CE) from the Villa Torlonia in Rome.

gateways. At the heart of the town there would be a forum flanked by public buildings—a temple, law courts, municipal edifices. Elsewhere, never too far from the town center, were public baths and an amphitheater—perhaps also a theater and even an *odeum* where musical performances were held. Such towns were focuses for Romanization, spreading Roman culture out into the surrounding countryside.

Yet for all the importance of the towns, it has been estimated that 90 percent of the Empire's population lived in the countryside, earning a living as smallholders or farm laborers. Many were slaves on the big agricultural estates, although the proportion declined over the years as landowners came to appreciate the cost savings involved in employing seasonal labor in their stead. Even as trade grew, the economy of the Empire remained primarily agricultural; most people's needs could be satisfied locally, and many practiced subsistence farming, providing all their own food themselves.

Farming and the countryside also, however, exerted a continuing pull on the imagination of town dwellers. Romans constantly harked back to the nation's early tradition of peasant landholding—a time that came to be seen nostalgically as a golden age. Amid the bustle of the capital's crowded streets, they hankered after a quiet rural life, much as modern commuters dream of a place in the country. The strain is often evident in Roman poetry: "Happy is the man who remains far from business and who cultivates the family farm with his own oxen," wrote Horace, himself the proud owner of a small estate in the Sabine Hills.

THE ROMAN STAGE

The chief form of entertainment in Rome other than gladiatorial shows was the theater. The impetus, as with so much of Rome's cultural life, came initially from Greece. The first true plays (as opposed to sketches and burlesques) ever performed in Rome were translations from the Greek, commissioned as part of the victory celebrations that marked the end of the First Punic War in 240BCE. Plays were originally staged in temporary wooden structures put up as part of the *ludi* ("games") that accompanied major religious festivals.

The genre that most appealed to the Roman audience was comedy and, more specifically, the works of the Greek dramatist Menander, as freely translated and adapted by the preeminent second-century BCE playwrights Plautus and Terence. Even so, their dramas had to compete with other attractions, not always successfully. In one of his plays, Terence complains of audiences drifting off to watch a tightrope walker, while the poet Horace bemoaned people interrupting performances to call for boxers or a bear.

More decorous entertainments were offered in the *odeums*—smaller, roofed auditoriums used for musical performances, lectures, and poetry readings. Free entertainment was also available in the law courts, where people flocked to hear celebrity lawyers practicing the rhetorical skills by which Romans set such store.

In the long run, Roman theater fell victim to competition from other forms of entertainment. The brutal diversions of the circus and the arena (see pages 82–85) sapped the taste for subtler pleasures. By the third century CE, most theaters were staging mimes, farces, or wild beast shows rather than dramas. Soon afterward, they fell silent altogether, and only the works of Plautus, Terence, and Seneca survived to keep alive the memory of the Roman stage.

RIGHT **A Roman theater (ca. 2nd century CE) in Bosra, Syria, the ancient capital of the province of Arabia. Like their Greek counterparts, Roman theaters were semicircular; spectators sat on banked rows of seats and gazed across an open space to the stage. In Rome, that space was occupied by senators and other patricians, sitting on folding chairs; the first rows of banked seats were reserved for other leading citizens. Most theaters were unroofed, but the spectators were protected from direct sunlight or rain by an awning. The actors were slaves or freedmen working for a manager commissioned by the organizer of the games.**

PERFORMANCE AND IDENTITY: THE MASK

Rome inherited theatrical masks from Greece; masks indicated to the audience the person being portrayed and let actors take more than one role within the same play and switch genders (the players were always men). Masks were also popular motifs: in a fresco (opposite) from a villa in Pompeii, 60–50 BCE, the head of Silenus is visible below a mask of his face; and the design of this 1st-century CE incense burner (above) was inspired by comedies in which slave characters could taunt their masters without fear of reprisal provided they were seated on an altar.

SPORT AND SPECTACLE

The satirist Juvenal complained that the average Roman citizens of his day only cared about bread and circuses, and the emperors certainly took pains to keep them well supplied with both. The circus, for Romans, meant above all the Circus Maximus, the capital's principal racetrack, which had room for at least 150,000 spectators. People flocked there to enjoy chariot racing, the most enduring of all the city's spectator entertainments. Like stage plays, the races formed part of the *ludi* (games) that accompanied public festivals; it has been estimated that in the mid-first century CE there was racing on eighty days each year.

Chariots were usually drawn by four horses. Their drivers competed over seven laps of a track that consisted of two long straights and two 180-degree bends; each lap covered about 5,000 feet (1,500 meters). The sport was dangerous, as vehicles often collided at the turns. A charioteer who lost control risked being crushed under horses' hooves or else being dragged to his death entangled in the reins, unless he could cut them with the small knife that each rider carried for that purpose.

In republican days, chariot teams were privately owned by wealthy individuals, but, under the emperors, they were managed by contractors identified by their racing colors: red, white, blue, or green. Each color had its band of eager partisans. Passions were further aroused by the heavy betting that accompanied the racing.

The risks that the charioteers ran were as nothing compared with those that faced gladiators. Gladiatorial contests came to Rome from Etruria, where they had their origins in sacrificial displays staged at public funerals to honor the memory of the dead. According to Livy, they were first introduced

BELOW A Roman gold model of a charioteer and his horses. Successful charioteers became heroes and could earn huge sums of money. An inscription has preserved the career record of one track star who won 1,462 of the 4,257 races in which he competed in the course of a career of 24 years. His earnings totalled 36 million *sesterces*—a sum a legionary would have taken 30,000 years to earn.

in the year 264BCE. Under the emperors, the fights came to challenge chariot racing as the capital's favorite entertainment. Five thousand pairs of gladiators are said to have fought in games held by the emperor Trajan in 107CE to celebrate his victory in the Dacian War.

Most gladiators were forced into the job as condemned criminals or prisoners of war, or else were sold into it as slaves. There were gladiatorial schools to train raw recruits in fighting skills; it was from one of these that Spartacus escaped in 73BCE to lead a slave revolt that defied the might of Rome for two years. Different types of gladiator reflected native fighting traditions in their skills: Thracians fought with a round shield and scimitar, while Samnites wore huge, visored helmets and wielded swords and oblong shields. The *murmillo* fought with similar equipment to the Samnite, but with a helmet bearing a metal fish as a crest, while the *retiarius*

ABOVE Detail from a 4th-century CE mosaic portraying a gladiator fighting a wild beast. In some of the more gruesome shows staged in Roman arenas, lions, tigers, or panthers were released to fight armed men; in other cases, naturally nonaggressive beasts were either goaded into fighting for their lives or were simply massacred.

went into the ring lightly clad with just a trident and a net, relying on agility to take on heavily armed opponents.

In theory, gladiators fought to the death; in practice, it was not always so. Records of a Pompeiian games show that only three of the nine losers died. A wounded gladiator would raise a hand to ask for mercy from the spectators. They, in turn, would hold up their hands with thumb and forefinger pressed together to signify clemency; if they raised their thumbs alone and pointed them at their breasts, they expected the death blow. It was up to the emperor or some other presiding dignitary to interpret their wishes and give the appropriate command.

Successful gladiators won their freedom, symbolized by the presentation of a wooden sword. They could also become popular heroes and even sex symbols: "Celadus the Thracian makes all the girls sigh," a graffito from Pompeii records. Another Pompeiian inscription speaks of one man winning his fifty-fifth bout, suggesting that successful fighters could have relatively long careers.

However brutal, the gladiatorial contests at least involved real skills. The same could not be said for some of the more ghastly spectactles staged in the arenas. Wild animals were slaughtered in huge numbers. According to Cicero, who attended a particularly bloody event in Rome, the crowd showed signs of revulsion at the treatment meted out, particularly to the elephants: "There was even an impulse of compassion," he noted, "a feeling that the beasts had something human about them." Such empathy had little long-term effect, for 3,500 elephants were subsequently killed in the arena under the emperor Augustus alone.

Worse still were the public executions that were carried out in the arenas in the guise of sport. Armed criminals were put in the ring unprotected to kill one another, a spectacle that the philosopher Seneca described as "murder pure and simple," or else were left to face wild beasts unarmed. Famously, Christians were

ABOVE **A young woman playing ball in the** *palaestra*, **or gymnasium; detail from a late 3rd- to early 4th-century** CE **mosaic in the Piazza Armerina or Villa Romana del Casale, Sicily.**

RIGHT **Spectator involvement in events such as chariot racing (shown here in a 2nd-century** CE **Gallo-Roman mosaic) was so intense that riots sometimes broke out in the arenas—especially when heavy betting was involved and supporters felt that their man had been fouled.**

among the victims—according to Tacitus, the emperor Nero had some wrapped in wild animal skins to be hunted down by dogs.

In the long run, the brutality of the gladiator and wild beast shows corrupted and degraded Roman taste, driving out other, more civilized forms of entertainment. In pandering to the worst instincts of the mob, the emperors debased their own culture and cast serious doubt on Rome's claim to moral superiority over the barbarian world beyond its borders.

THE COLOSSEUM

Known as the Flavian Amphitheater in antiquity, the Colosseum (right) got its present name, after the western Empire's collapse, from a colossal statue of the emperor Nero that stood nearby. The vast stadium was built on the orders of the emperor Vespasian in a central location to the east of the Roman Forum; its construction formed part of a general embellishment of the capital designed to restore morale after the chaos of the "Year of the Four Emperors" (see page 12).

The building took the form of a gigantic oval more than 320,000 square feet (30,000 square meters) in extent, with the central arena alone covering more than 51,000 square feet (nearly 5,000 square meters). It was officially inaugurated by Vespasian's successor, Titus, in 80CE, with a spectacle whose scale and brutality set the scene for what was to follow: some 5,000 wild animals, kept in underground cages, were killed in the opening days, and another 4,000 over the next three months. The Empire's best-known gladiators fought here, and the entire central arena could be flooded for the staging of mock sea battles.

The Colosseum remained in use to the very end of the western Empire and was even restored by Odoacer, the Germanic general who replaced the last of the emperors. It finally fell into disuse in the sixth century, partly as a result of the Christian church's disapproval of the shedding of blood for pleasure.

CHILDREN
OF MARS

LEFT In this cameo of 20CE, Aeneas, the legendary founder of the people of Rome and divine ancestor of the Julio-Claudian emperors, is shown bearing a globe (top left), in company with his descendants. Behind him, wearing a veil, is Augustus (or possibly Julius Caesar), while astride a winged horse rides Germanicus, one of Rome's finest soldiers. In the center section, the emperor Tiberius and his mother Livia sit enthroned, surrounded by other living members of their family, including Nero and Caligula. Below are subjugated barbarian captives, symbolizing the might of Rome.

F act and legend became inextricably entwined in Rome's early history. Its most famous names—Aeneas, Horatius, and Romulus and Remus (the children of Mars)—may or may not have existed, but all passed into later Roman chronicles as actual figures who helped shape their people's destiny. Such well-remembered incidents as the abduction of the Sabine women and the rape of Lucretia may similarly have served to dramatize real events in Rome's infancy. Yet for all their topicality, the legends have more than just local significance. The acts of heroism and violence of which they speak have a universal resonance that has kept them fresh in people's minds around the world to the present day.

BELOW A two-handled Roman cup in silver, 1st century CE, depicting a scene from the *Odyssey* by Homer. Odysseus, shown with raised sword, sacrifices a ram to summon the spirit of the blind seer, Teiresias (seated, left), in the hope that the seer will help him to return home.

THE WANDERINGS OF AENEAS

From early on, the Romans felt that the extraordinary destiny of their race required an exceptional founder. Their real origins stretched back well beyond the written record, leaving the field open to myth. Several different names were offered up, particularly by Greek historians who often chose to portray Rome as one of the many colonies set up in Italy by Greek emigrés in the dark ages after 1000BCE. The names that cropped up most often in these sources were Evander and Pallas—this last a youth whose name was later commemorated in Rome's Palatine Hill.

ABOVE **The great poet Virgil, author of the *Aeneid*, which tells the story of the origin of Rome, is portrayed in this mosaic from the 3rd century CE.**

The thought of a Greek origin was less attractive to Romans, particularly after Rome went to war with Greece in the third century BCE. Increasingly, they looked to another venerable figure long associated with the Latium region. This was Aeneas, best remembered today as the hero of Virgil's great national epic, the *Aeneid*.

The Aeneas legend long predated Virgil, who wrote in the reign of the emperor Augustus. Aeneas is mentioned in Homer's *Iliad*, not as a Greek hero but as a Trojan, second only to Hector in fighting skill. From about 525BCE on, Aeneas also became a familiar figure in Italy, featuring in artworks produced for the Etruscans, often by Greek craftsmen. Rome was under Etruscan rule at the time, so his name must have become well known in the city from that point. The tradition that Aeneas was the founder, not of Rome itself (an honor accorded to his distant successor Romulus) but of the Roman people, was thus well established before Virgil gave it canonical form.

The *Aeneid* describes how Aeneas, son of the mortal Anchises and the goddess Venus, escapes the destruction of Troy carrying his aged father on his back. He also

RIGHT **A 1st-century CE Pompeiian fresco depicting an episode from the *Aeneid* in which the wounded Aeneas has the point of an arrow extracted from his leg. His mother, Venus (left), watches on, while Aeneas's son, Ascanius, stands weeping at his side.**

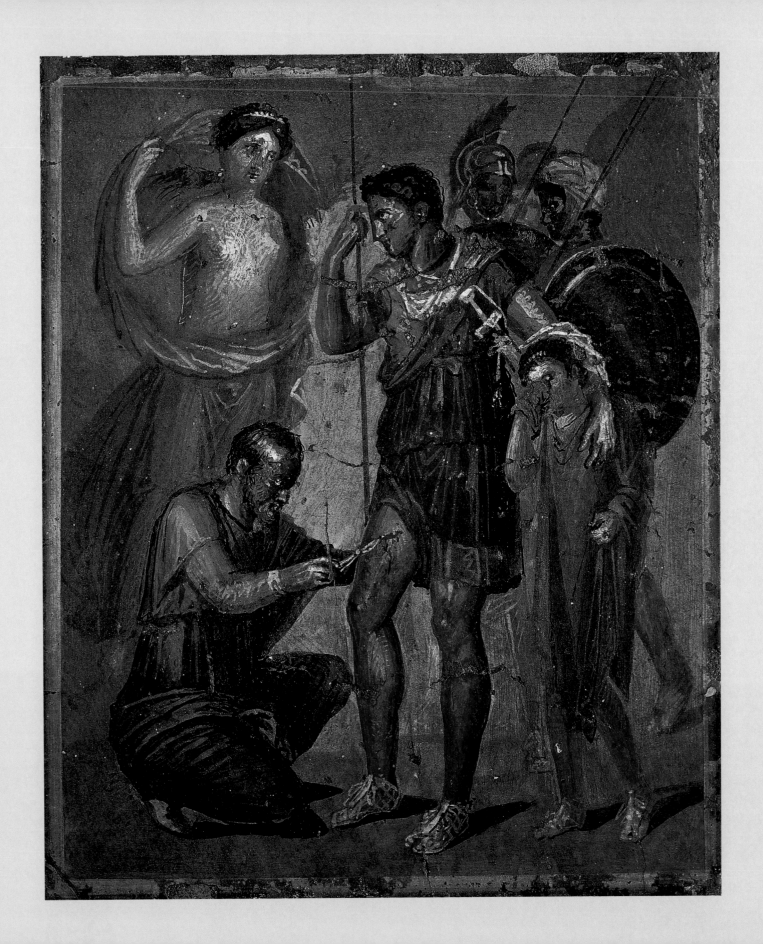

takes with him his household gods, transported in a portable shrine, and his son Ascanius, although his wife Creusa dies during their flight from the burning city. Aeneas then sails off with other survivors in search of a new homeland. The exiles travel first to Thrace, then to the Greek island of Delos, home of a famous oracle of the god Apollo. There they are told to seek out "the land of their forefathers"—a place they at first wrongly identify as Crete. After an unsuccessful attempt to settle on the island, however, Aeneas's household gods whisper to him the truth, that the Trojans' ancestors in fact originally came from the Latium region of Italy.

The journey to Latium is cursed by continual hostile interventions by the goddess Juno, sworn enemy of the Trojans. The seafarers have to survive terrifying encounters with legendary monsters of classical mythology—the bird-headed Harpies, gigantic Cyclopes, the murderous Scylla and Charybdis. They are also frequently diverted from their route, first to Sicily, where Anchises dies, and then to Carthage, where Aeneas is tempted to abandon his quest for the love of the Carthaginian queen Dido. Only divine intervention in the form of a message from Jupiter himself persuades him to abandon his lover in pursuit of his high destiny.

The first part of the *Aeneid*, describing the Trojans' wanderings, recalls Homer's *Odyssey*, which also recounts the tribulations of a hero traveling from the Trojan War. The second part, telling of the Trojans' arrival in Italy and the struggle to win a homeland, is closer to the *Iliad* in spirit. The hinge between the two sections is a lengthy description of Aeneas's journey to the Underworld in company with the Sibyl of Cumae (see pages 128–129). There Aeneas encounters the spirit of his father Anchises, who prophesies the future glory of the Roman race, culminating in the triumphant reign of Virgil's sponsor, Augustus.

Yet, thanks to the machinations of Juno, the Trojans' arrival in Latium at first brings nothing but strife. Turnus, king of the native Rutulian people, raises an army

to resist the newcomers, and bitter warfare follows, culminating when the leaders of the opposing armies meet in single combat. Only by killing his rival is Aeneas able at last to fulfil his destiny and provide his people with the promised new home.

The *Aeneid* ends abruptly with the heroes' duel in which Aeneas is successful and secures Rome's future, but references earlier in the poem already imply the subsequent course of events. Inspired by Father Tiber, the spirit of Rome's river, Aeneas sought out an omen, a white sow with thirty piglets, that marked the site where the Trojans were to settle. The place chosen was Lavinium, known today as the small town of Pratica di Mare, some 15 miles (25km) southeast of Rome. There Aeneas duly built a city, and there he finally died, having devoted his last years to merging his Trojans with the local Latin peoples. Subsequently, he won the ultimate accolade his achievements demanded, being worshipped as a god, Jupiter Indiges—the local Jove.

ROMULUS AND REMUS

Of all the Roman myths, few are as rich in folklore as that of Rome's founders, Romulus and Remus. The stories tell how two brothers, Amulius and Numitor, were jointly ruling Alba Longa—a city founded by Aeneas's son Ascanius—when one, Amulius, grew jealous over the succession. Staging a palace coup, he had Numitor imprisoned and forced his daughter, Rhea Silvia, to become a priestess of the goddess Vesta, thereby condemning her to perpetual virginity. But Rhea was subsequently violated, supposedly by the god Mars, and bore twin boys, Romulus and Remus.

Furious, Amulius ordered that the mother should be buried alive and the babies drowned in the Tiber. But the servants charged with the deed took pity on the twins and instead set them afloat in their cradle. The stream carried them ashore, where their crying attracted the attention of a she-wolf. Far from eating them, she suckled them with her own milk, sustaining them until human help arrived in the form of a shepherd, who put the boys in his wife's care.

The twins grew up strong and healthy and, on reaching manhood, won a reputation for bravery by attacking bandits who were preying on the shepherds. Word of their deeds reached Amulius, and they were summoned before him. At last their true identity was revealed, whereupon Romulus summarily dispatched the tyrant who had had his mother killed and restored Numitor to his rightful place on the throne.

The theme of twins suckled by animals also featured in Greek mythology, and so was probably already known to the Etruscans before it became attached to Rome's founders. This splendid bronze wolf (see illustration, right), now in Rome's Capitoline Museum, was cast in Etruria in about the fifth century BCE, and may well have originally had nothing to do with the Romulus legend. The figures of the twins were only added much later, when the statue was rediscovered in Renaissance times, turning the work into an iconic image of Rome's legendary beginnings.

THE BIRTH OF ROME

T he legend of Aeneas explained the origins of the Roman people but not of Rome itself. There was a quasi-historical reason for this discrepancy, for, by the time that the legends were written down, people realized that there was a chronological gap to fill between the two events. Troy was thought to have fallen in the twelfth century BCE, while Rome was not founded until the eighth century—tradition set the date at 753BCE.

To fill the gap, legend provided two separate precursor cities: Aeneas's foundation, Lavinium, and Alba Longa, established by his son Ascanius. A line of fourteen kings was sketched in—they were said to have occupied the Alban throne before the twin grandsons of the king decided to build a city of their own. But the relationship between Rome's founders, Romulus and Remus (see page 94), turned murderous even before the city was completed. Romulus killed Remus, supposedly in a fit of anger when Remus belittled the town's defenses by jumping over a wall. "So die anyone else who scorns these walls!" Romulus shouted as he delivered the fatal blow.

Even when the walls were complete, the city's future was by no means secure, not least because of a lack of women to bear fresh generations of Romans. So Romulus invited the neighboring Sabine people to attend a festival in the newly completed city, and then set the young men of Rome loose on them. Each youth snatched a girl from the arms of her helpless parents—then over the ensuing months did his best to soothe the outraged feelings of his unwilling bride.

The Rape of the Sabine Women caused a legacy of bitterness between the two communities that eventually led to war. At first the Sabine forces sought to penetrate Rome's defenses in vain. Eventually, however, they found a young Roman girl, Tarpeia, who agreed to open a gate for them.

RIGHT Legend tells how, following a family feud, Rhea Silvia was condemned by her uncle, Amulius, to a life of perpetual virginity. The plan was thwarted, however, by the appearance of the great god of war, Mars, who impregnated her and for whom she subsequently bore twin boys, Romulus and Remus, who later became the founders of the city of Rome. The stone relief shown here, ca. 100BCE–300CE, was discovered at Aquincum in Hungary and depicts Mars appearing to Rhea Silvia.

With the enemy inside the gates, war to the death threatened. It was averted, however, by the Sabine women, who had eventually come to care for their husbands, as well as for the parents from whom they had been so cruelly separated. They threw themselves between the opposing armies, appealing to both sides for peace. The soldiers recognized the justice of their demand, and a truce was arranged. In time, the pact developed into a lasting alliance that saw Romulus and the Sabine leader Tatius jointly ruling a combined realm. The moral of the tale was clear: Rome had come to stay, and its future lay in friendly alliance with the neighboring peoples.

TYRANTS AND LAWGIVERS

BELOW Numa Pompilius, one of the most capable of the six kings who followed the reign of Romulus, is said to have introduced the cult of the vestal virgins, priestesses of the goddess Vesta. Their duties included maintaining the sacred fire in the Temple of Vesta in the Roman Forum. In this 1st-century CE stone relief, Vesta (seated) is shown with four of her vestal virgins.

According to legend, Rome had six kings after Romulus: respectively, Numa Pompilius, Tullus Hostilius, Ancus Martius, Tarquinius Priscus, Servius Tullius, and Tarquinius Superbus ("Tarquin the Proud"). There was an almost schematic pattern to their tenures of power. The first, third, and fifth—Numa, Ancus, and Servius—were capable leaders and had, for the most part, long and peaceful reigns.

The reigns of the other three kings were marked by upheaval. Numa's successor, Tullus, was a warrior, and under his stewardship Rome was almost constantly at war. This was the time when the city finally conquered its neighbor and predecessor Alba Longa, and one of the most enduring Roman legends grew up around the struggle. It was said that, rather than fight a pitched battle, the two communities agreed to put their fate in the hands of champions. Each army had triplets in its ranks: the Horatii brothers on the Roman side, the Curiatii for the Albans. In the ensuing hand-to-hand encounter, two of the Horatii were quickly killed, but not before wounding their opponents. The third realized that his best chance of survival lay in facing his enemies one at a time rather than together, and so pretended to flee. The Curiatii straggled out in pursuit of him, at which point he turned and killed the foremost. The other two in turn received the same treatment, leaving him and Rome masters of the field.

Tarquinius Priscus, Rome's fourth king, was the first of the city's Etruscan rulers—although, according to the historian Livy, his ethnic background was actually Greek. Nonetheless, Tarquin originally bore the Etruscan name Lucumo, and traveled to Rome with his

RIGHT Lucius Junius Brutus, aristocratic founder of the Republic and model of the stern, patriotic Roman republican, is portrayed in this late 4th-century BCE bronze bust. Brutus was at the forefront of the revolt against Tarquin, which eventually brought about the downfall of the monarchy (see page 100).

wife Tanaquil from the Etruscan city of Tarquinia. An ambitious man, he won the trust of the king, Ancus Martius, who made him guardian of his own children. Then, when Ancus died, he sent his wards, the legitimate heirs to the empty throne, on a hunting expedition and, in their absence, had himself pronounced king.

Despite his deviousness, Tarquin was an effective ruler, and Rome's borders expanded under his rule. However, Ancus's sons never forgave the usurpation, and many years later they engineered his assassination. Even then the throne did not pass to them, for Tarquin's widow Tanaquil managed to ensure that his adopted heir, Servius, was chosen in their stead. Servius had been favored by Tarquin, partly as a

result of a portent: he had been found one day in the palace with a ring of fire around his head. Tanaquil, who had Etruscan powers of divination, immediately foresaw a great future for him and persuaded Tarquin to bring him up as his heir, preferring his claim even to that of their own two sons.

For all his abilities, Servius also came to a violent end—in his case, at the hands of one of the heirs he had supplanted. Tarquin the Proud, a son or grandson of the earlier Tarquin, was married to Tullia, a daughter of Servius who was quite as ambitious as he was. In Servius's old age, this unfilial child persuaded her husband to stage a coup, in the course of which Servius was killed. Legend then insists that Tullia, who had already had her first husband killed to marry Tarquin, drove her chariot over her father's body as it lay in the street.

Tarquin and Tullia were the Macbeth and Lady Macbeth of Roman history: able, maybe, but vitiated by unscrupulous ambition. Tarquin's ruthlessness was such that he came to be hated as a tyrant; he was also resented by later generations of Romans for the period of Etruscan domination that he represented. His downfall was intimately linked to the tale of the rape of Lucretia. The story tells that two of the king's sons were boasting one night of the respective merits of their wives while in the company of a young nobleman, Collatinus. Drunkenly, the three decided to ride to the capital to compare the ladies' merits at first hand. They found the two royal brides socializing at parties, while Collatinus's wife, Lucretia, was at home demurely spinning—an appropriate occupation for a Roman matron. One of Tarquin's sons, Sextus, returned to Lucretia's house a few days later and violated her in the middle of the night at swordpoint. Lucretia sent for her father and her husband, who arrived in company with Lucius Junius Brutus, a nephew of Tarquin. She demanded vengeance, then plunged a knife into her breast. Word of the crime spread through Rome, acting as a catalyst for revolt among a people already sorely oppressed by Tarquin's rule. With Brutus at the head of the mob, the monarchy was eventually brought down, and with it the period of Etruscan domination.

CITIZEN HEROES

A whole cycle of legends built up around the first years of the Republic, most of them concerned with Tarquin the Proud's attempts to regain the throne—and there were several such. At first he tried conspiracy, plotting with influential Romans to engineer his return. Among the conspirators were two sons of Rome's liberator, Brutus; and, noble Roman that he was, he stoically watched their execution when they were condemned to death for their treason. Next, Tarquin allied with the Etruscan cities of Tarquinia and Veii to win back power by force. Again Brutus frustrated him, this time riding out to confront Tarquin's son, Aruns, in single combat. Both died in the ensuing duel, but the Republic was saved.

Tarquin's third attempt was made in conjunction with Lars Porsena of Clusium. This time republican Rome owed its survival to the heroism of Horatius Cocles, who, with two companions, held the wooden bridge across the Tiber River against the invading army while defenders hacked away its supports. When it

LEFT **Julius Caesar (100–44BCE) is shown in this 1st-century sculpture with all the gravitas, or high seriousness, befitting a Roman hero. A brilliant military leader and a talented historian, Caesar was eventually brought down by his own ambition. His appointment as dictator for life aroused the bitter hostility of his political opponents. On March 15, 44BCE, a group of 60 conspirators who claimed to be acting in the spirit of republican virtue—and led by Marcus Junius Brutus, descendant of Lucius Junius Brutus, one of the republic's founders—struck down the general they believed was intent on bringing the Republic to an end.**

finally collapsed, he hurled himself fully armed into the stream, successfully swimming through a hail of missiles back to the Roman bank.

Having failed to take the city by assault, Porsena then settled in to besiege it. Again he was confounded by indomitable republican courage. A certain Caius Mucius had himself smuggled into the Etruscan camp, where he attempted to assassinate the Etruscan leader, but mistakenly killed his secretary instead. Taken before Porsena, he was ordered to name his fellow conspirators under threat of torture, but voluntarily thrust his right hand into the fire to show the impossibility of forcing him to speak. Porsena was so impressed by his valor that he withdrew his forces, leaving Tarquin to eke out a lonely old age in the Greek colony of Cumae, his hopes of restoration finally put to rest.

The legendary figures of later republican times were more ambiguous in their heroism than these early champions. The best remembered now is probably Coriolanus, thanks to Shakespeare's play of the same name. Coriolanus won his title of honor by conquering the town of Corioli from the Volscians in the course of a fifth-century-BCE war. However, he lost popular support by refusing to distribute corn to the people during a period of famine and was forced into exile. In his anger, he offered his services to the very Volscians he had earlier defeated, and in due course led a Volscian army almost to the gates of Rome. There he was met by his wife and his mother, who appealed to his patriotism not to attack his own city. Moved, he called off the attack and was later put to death by the Volscians for failing to press home the assault.

Similar clouds hung over the career of Camillus, hero of the ten-year siege of Veii, the last independent Etruscan city, which finally fell to the Romans in 396BCE. For all his services to the nation, he was accused of appropriating booty from the conquered city, and he, too, went into exile. However, his story had a happy ending. He was recalled to Rome to lead resistance to the Gauls, who captured the city in 390BCE, and lived to regain the glory of which he had been unjustly deprived.

LEGENDS OF THE EMPERORS

From the third century BCE on, Rome's history is richer in factual drama than in legend. Roman culture included several notable historians, and even if Livy, Tacitus, Sallust, and others were occasionally guilty of romanticizing the past, they nonetheless set a standard of rational enquiry for future generations to follow.

One of the few incidents in later Roman history that possessed a genuinely legendary aura was the so-called Rain Miracle, which took place around 174CE in Marcus Aurelius's reign. It was the time of the first major barbarian incursions into the Empire, when Germanic peoples swept south across the Danube frontier. A Roman detachment was trapped by its enemies in a narrow defile. The soldiers were running out of water and seemed on the verge of disaster when a lightning bolt spread terror in the opposing ranks. Rain then miraculously poured down, giving the dispirited legionaries new heart to attack their opponents, whom they put to flight.

LEFT A sudden rainstorm that fell upon Roman soldiers fighting in 174CE, in what is now Slovakia, saved them from death— it was so timely that they regarded it as miraculous. Known as the Rain Miracle, the event was recorded for posterity on the triumphal marble column (illustrated here) that Marcus Aurelius erected in Rome in the 2nd century CE, where a god, possibly Jupiter, is shown sending the downpour.

The wilder stories that attached themselves to the emperors sometimes smacked more of backstairs gossip than of legend properly so called. In fact, given that the imperial succession sometimes put absolute power in the hands of immature adolescents, many were no doubt true. Suetonius, for example, detailed his subjects' sexual excesses. Caligula, he claimed, had incestuous relations with all three of his sisters and forced two of them to have relations with his friends. Attending the wedding of a leading nobleman, he had the bride carried off for his own enjoyment. When his extravagance left him strapped for cash, he opened a brothel in his palace, stocking it with respectable married women and freeborn young men. In a similar vein, Nero is said to have married a young man named Sporus in a wedding ceremony complete with bridal veil and dowry. He liked to dress in animal skins and be penned in a cage, from which he was released to maul male and female victims who were bound to stakes in the manner of Christians in the arena.

Such stories contributed hugely to the most enduring of all Roman legends—that of the Empire's own decadence. As a corrective, it is important to remember that Caligula and Nero were exceptions—most emperors were hard-working soldiers without whose tireless efforts the Roman *imperium* would never have survived for almost 500 years.

RIGHT **A portrait head of the emperor Caligula, ca. 40CE. Many tales circulated about the bizarre antics of this ruler. The historian Suetonius claimed that he kept his favorite horse, Incitatus, in an ivory stall in a marble stable and provided it with a house, complete with slaves and furniture, in which to entertain guests whom the emperor invited in its name. Caligula was also said to enjoy wallowing in gold pieces.**

EMPERORS AS GODS

The Greek myths presented the Romans not just with great stories but also parables of power that could be used to boost the imperial image. Every emperor sought to present himself as the supreme authority, broadcasting his name on coins that circulated around the empire (above, left and right). Others went further, identifying with superhuman heroes of mythology. Here, a 1st-century CE sculptor (opposite) depicts Claudius as the god Jupiter, while Commodus (above; reigned 180–192CE) in this 2nd-century CE bust, has deliberately styled himself as Hercules, a conceit that contributed to his assassination.

THE DIVINE SPHERE

"We Romans owe our supremacy over all other peoples to our piety and religious observances and to our wisdom in believing that the spirit of the gods rules and directs everything." Or so claimed the orator Cicero. Yet Roman religion had little of the passion that has characterized other lands and other faiths. In their beliefs, as in most other spheres, the Romans were, above all, practical, seeking direct, visible benefits in return for their efforts. Observance started in the home, where the father of the family carried out daily rituals designed to ensure good fortune. Similarly, the state cult sought to win the favor of the gods for Rome as a whole through the performance of age-old rites whose origins were largely lost in the mists of time.

THE ROMAN PANTHEON

R ome's gods present a paradox: they are as familiar as song lyrics or planet names, but are also surprisingly little known. Most Western schoolchildren have heard of Venus, if not also of Jupiter, Mars, Mercury, and Saturn. Yet the origins of these deities, and what is specifically Roman about them, continue to puzzle scholars.

The roots of this problem lay in Rome's avid assimilation of all things Greek, including the Greek gods. Its own divinities were shadowy and insubstantial in comparison with the larger-than-life players in the Olympian soap opera. Accordingly, their native identities quickly became subsumed within the personas of the Hellenic imports. So Jupiter, as we know him from Roman literary sources, is Zeus by another name; Mercury took on the attributes of Hermes, the messenger of Mount Olympos (the home of the gods); Neptune, the sea god, became identified with the Greek Poseidon, and Vulcan, the divine blacksmith, with Hephaistos. At least one major Roman deity, Apollo, had no native counterpart, and therefore retained his Greek name.

Tracking down the Roman gods' own identities is difficult as the evidence lies hidden in preliterate times. The earliest surviving sources are annotations found on religious calendars and ritual formulas that were probably enigmatic even to the people who used them. Current knowledge suggests,

LEFT **Jupiter, the supreme lord of the heavens and head of the Roman pantheon, is shown in this marble statue of the 1st century CE as a mature, bearded man. He would originally have held in his hands a thunderbolt and a scepter, attributes linked to his identification with thunder and to his role as king of the gods.**

however, that Jupiter, addressed in later times as *optimus maximus* ("best and greatest"), started life as a typical Indo-European sky god, comparable to the Norse deity Thor or the Hittite god Teshub, and probably arrived in Rome with the Iron Age immigrants who also brought with them the Latin language. Augurs searched the heavens for omens of his pleasure or displeasure, and he was particularly identified with thunderstorms: the Thunderer was one of his epithets. The Etruscans had a similar divinity, Tinia, whom they associated with two goddesses, Uni and Menrva; these three, Romanized as Jupiter, Juno, and Minerva, were the presiding deities of Rome's best-known early temple, founded under the Etruscan kings.

In later times, when Jupiter also became associated with the Greek god Zeus, he took on Zeus's attributes as ruler of the universe. He was portrayed as a divine father figure who epitomized good faith, honor, and justice, and Romans swore their most binding oaths in his name. He was also the protector of Rome and the Roman people, invoked by consuls before any military expedition and always rewarded with a share of the spoils.

The preeminent Roman war god, however, was Mars. As befitted the patron of a military people, he occupied a markedly higher place in the pantheon than his Greek equivalent Ares, ranking second only to Jupiter in status. Along with Jupiter, he was one of a trio of gods worshipped above all others in pre-Etruscan days; the third in the trio was Quirinus, a now largely forgotten Sabine deity whose name is commemorated in Rome's Quirinal Hill, where his cult was centered.

Mars started life as a fertility god who presided over the spring equinox; the link lingers linguistically in the month name of March. The main feasts in his honor were held at that time, when a body of priests named the Salians dressed in military uniform to perform a leaping dance intended to encourage new growth—a rite that combined Mars's martial and agricultural aspects. Legend credited him as the

ABOVE **A marble statue (Rome, 100–200CE) of Apollo, son of Jupiter, twin brother of the goddess Diana, and god of, among other things, music and prophecy. At his feet are the remnants of a griffin, a mythological creature with which he was associated.**

father of Romulus and Remus, emphasizing his role as a founder of the Roman state. The Campus Martius ("Field of Mars"), where the oldest altar to Mars was sited, was the Roman army's traditional gathering place.

If Mars was sacred to farmers and warriors, Mercury was the patron of merchants and tradesmen. His cult always tended to appeal more to ordinary people than to the ruling classes and was centered around his temple, which was situated on Rome's Aventine Hill, in the plebeian quarter of the city. The god's Greek equivalent, Hermes, was the messenger of the gods, and Mercury himself took on this role in later Roman tradition. The adjective "mercurial" is suggestive of the speed with which he carried out his various missions.

One native god who possessed no Greek equivalent was Janus, the two-faced guardian of doors and entrances and the patron of beginnings. Fittingly, his name lives on in the month of January, the first month of the year, when his feast was celebrated. An ancient god, he was reputed to have helped Rome repel an attack on the Capitol, and the gates of his temple in the Forum were ever after left open in time of war. This therefore meant that they were rarely closed over the course of Rome's long and battle-scarred history, although the emperor Augustus made a point of shutting them when, in 29BCE, he finally restored peace to the Empire after decades of bitter civil strife.

One version of Roman myth claimed that Janus had once jointly ruled the world with Saturn, a contradictory deity who became associated with the Greek Chronos. On the one hand, Saturn was a god of wine and revelry, celebrated in the great festival

LEFT A stele (323CE), from Roman provincial territory in North Africa, dedicated to Saturn, a god of agriculture, wine, and revelry whose annual festival, the Saturnalia, was held in December (see page 121).

RIGHT The Temple of Antoninus and Faustina was built (ca. 141CE) by emperor Antoninus Pius (reigned 138–161CE) to honor his deified wife, Faustina. Antoninus Pius's successors, Marcus Aurelius and Lucius Verus, later erected a marble column in honor of their deified predecessor and his wife. The base of the column, shown here, portrays a winged *genius* (guardian spirit) and two eagles escorting the deified couple (top, center) to heaven. Personifications (bottom, right and left) of Rome and the Campus Martius look on.

known as the Saturnalia (see pages 120–121); on the other, he was a gloomy melancholic, possessing all the qualities conveyed by the word "saturnine." For patriotic Roman mythographers, however, he and Janus together presided over a golden age that saw the introduction of agriculture and all the arts of civilization. And, unsurprisingly, in the light of Roman civic patriotism, they were said to have spread these gifts to humankind not just from Italy, but from the banks of the Tiber River, not far from the spot where Rome itself would one day stand.

THE GREAT GODDESSES

Early Romans seem not to have been overworried by the gender of their deities. The formula *si deus si dea*—"whether god or goddess"—crops up in several dedications, indicating uncertainty as to the sex of some of the lesser divinities. In later times, though, the great goddesses acquired vivid personalities that between them spanned the spectrum of femininity known to the Roman world. Thus Jupiter's consort, Juno, represented the idealized Roman matron, full of dignity and authority. Ceres stood for fertility, Venus for sexual desire, while Diana the huntress was a model of tomboyish independence, with even a hint of lesbianism in her persona. As for Minerva, she was wisdom and creativity personified, a lofty and remote presence.

As usual in Roman mythology, there were contradictions within the general picture: the vengeful Juno of Virgil's *Aeneid*, mercilessly dogging the hero's path to Italy, was hardly matronly, no doubt because her portrayal there leaned heavily on traditions of her Greek counterpart, Hera. The Roman goddess Juno seems originally to have been a moon deity, but came eventually to be seen as a protector of women, particularly associated with childbirth and with marriage; her

LEFT **The so-called Juno Ludovisi, a beautiful head of the goddess Juno, originally part of a colossal statue, ca. 1st century BCE. Geese consecrated to Juno warned Rome's citizens of a Gaulish nighttime attack on the Capitol in 390BCE, earning her the title of "Juno Moneta," the giver of warnings. As the first Roman coins were produced in the temple of Juno Moneta, the word came to be attached first to mints and then to the currency they produced, an association that still survives in the word "money."**

———114———

RIGHT Diana, goddess of the hunt, was worshipped extensively in ancient Rome, and many temples were erected in her honor, including one on the Aventine Hill in Rome, with others in the provinces. She is portrayed in this 1st-century CE Pompeiian fresco in full hunting regalia.

festal month of June was regarded as a propitious one for weddings.

The roles assigned to the other goddesses were more specific. Ceres, for example, started life as an ancient Italian grain goddess. The deity presiding over crops and vegetation, she was honored in a springtime festival, the Cerealia, and her name lingers on in the English word "cereal." Minerva seems originally to have been an Etruscan divinity and was the protectress of several Etruscan city-states. Later, however, she became linked with the Greek Athene, who sprang fully armed from the head of Zeus, and the connection led her sometimes to be regarded as a war goddess. Mostly, though, she was associated with arts and crafts, and as such was the patron of craftsmen and of all who lived by their wits, among them writers, schoolmasters, and doctors.

Venus, the love goddess, had unlikely origins as the presiding spirit of vegetable gardens. Initially, she was purely Roman, although in time she became confounded with the Etruscan Turan and the Greek Aphrodite, emerging as the divine beauty familiar in Western culture from the paintings of Botticelli and others. For Romans, however, she had another role as the mother of Aeneas and was worshipped as the goddess of desire among the population at large as Genetrix, the pious begetter of the state.

A SHRINE FOR ALL THE GODS

The emperor Hadrian ordered the construction of a Pantheon early in the second century CE as a sanctuary dedicated to all the gods. The resultant temple's *rotunda* design was an engineering masterpiece, with its revolutionary dome (see illustration, right) remaining the world's largest until modern times. The diameter exactly matches the height of the topmost point above the temple's floor, lending the building a sense of harmony that led the poet Shelley, who visited in the early nineteenth century, to speak of "the perfection of its proportions."

Shelley also likened the roof to "the unmeasured dome of Heaven," a comparison that may well have come close to the builders' original intentions. No records survive to name the architect or outline his vision, but scholars believe that statues of gods associated with the sky—Jupiter, Mercury, Mars, Venus—were placed in the niches that ring the building's inner wall. The dome itself, which was coffered (patterned with symmetrical recesses) to reduce its overall weight, probably represented the firmament. Its top was left open to allow light to filter through. This aperture, known as the *oculus*, or eye, symbolized the sun, whose radiance bathed the interior of the building.

The engineers who constructed the Pantheon did their job well. The temple survived the fall of paganism to become a Christian church in 609CE. It remains there to this day and is often considered the finest intact example of ancient Roman architecture, with its original dome and internal columns still in place.

SPIRITS OF THE HOME

Every Roman household, however poor, had its guardian spirits who were honored daily. In return for the attention and respect paid to them, they protected the fortunes of the family and ensured that they had food on the table. These protectors came in several different forms. The *lares* were generally thought of as spirits of departed ancestors. The most important was the *lar familiaris*, who represented the founder of the family; Aeneas and Romulus occupied this position for the Roman state. The *penates* took their name from the *penus*, or pantry, in which food was stored, and their particular duty was to ensure that the family received its daily bread. The first fruits of the harvest were offered up to them, and the salt cellar placed on the dining table stood there in their honor. The superstitions that linger to this day about spilling salt stem from this custom—the *penates*, who might have considered such accidents marks of disrespect, needed to be placated by the offering of a pinch of the spilled salt, traditionally cast over the diner's left shoulder.

The *lares* and *penates* were jointly worshipped at a small shrine that had pride of place in most Roman living rooms. It could take the form of a stone altar, typically inscribed with an image of the *genius* (spirit) of the house flanked by two *lares*;

RIGHT A household shrine in the House of Menander, Pompeii, Italy. Images of family ancestors are displayed in a recess in the wall set behind an altar. It was customary in ancient Rome for the head of the household to say a prayer each day before such shrines and to leave small offerings of wine and incense.

alternatively, it might be a cupboard containing small statues of the gods made of gold, silver, ivory, or clay, depending on the family's means. The other main focus of family worship was the hearth—the Latin word for it was in fact *focus*. It was sacred to the goddess Vesta, an ancient Italian fire deity. The connection probably went back to early times, when the farmers who first set up their dwellings on the hills of Rome would gather each evening around the fire in the center of their circular huts, drawn by the warmth in winter and by the scent of meat roasting. In later times, offerings of food and wine were left on the hearth, as at the family shrine, or were thrown into the fire itself.

There were also public versions of these ubiquitous household deities. *Lares compitales* ("*lares* of the crossroads") were propitiated at shrines marking the boundaries between several farms, in the countryside, or between neighborhoods, in towns. As for Vesta, she was one of Rome's best-known divinities, venerated in a beautiful circular temple in the Forum where her sacred flame was always kept alight. The six Vestal Virgins, chosen from the best families and vowed to chastity for the thirty years they dedicated to the goddess's service, were among the nation's most honored citizens. They risked being buried alive if they were found to have fallen short of their vows; but in the millennium for which the institution survived, only eighteen are said to have suffered this terrible fate.

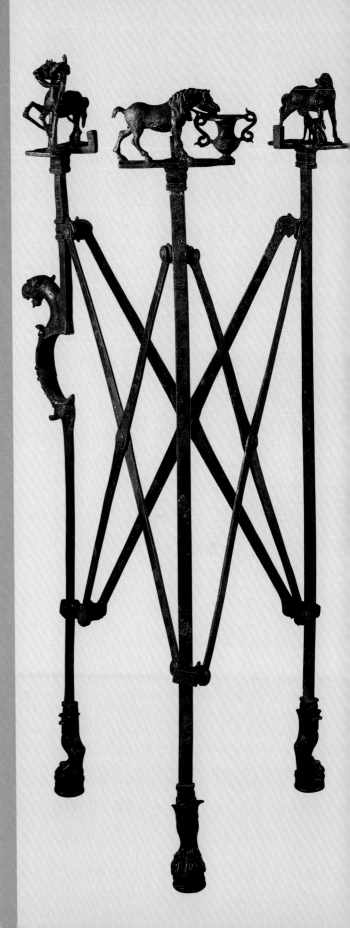

GODS OF FEASTS AND FESTIVALS

Public worship in the Roman world centered around the state festivals, which dated back to very ancient times. The earliest known ritual calendar, ascribed to the reign of Romulus's supposed heir Numa Pompilius (see page 98), already listed forty-five of them. Later, festal inflation set in. The total had risen to sixty-six feast days by the end of the Republic, to 135 by the second-century CE reign of Marcus Aurelius (who cut the number back), and to a colossal 175 days near the Empire's end in 354CE. The early festivals addressed the needs of an agricultural society, seeking to ensure the goodwill of the gods—Romans called it the *pax deorum* ("peace of the gods"). Over the centuries, however, they lost much of their original religious significance and became public holidays pure and simple, celebrated with games in the arenas and with theater shows. Priests continued to perform the timeworn rituals in the temples, but in later years they were often unaware of the true meaning of the formulas that tradition had passed on to them.

Many of the more ancient Latin gods had festivals dedicated to them. At the Cerealia, the springtime celebration in honor of Ceres (see pages 114–115), married women gave up drink and marital relations for a week and took part in torchlit nighttime processions. Pales, a deity of flocks and shepherds, was honored in the Parilia, celebrated in late April. A late-summer carousal was dedicated to Consus and Ops, Italian harvest gods. One god invoked less than his modern-day reputation might suggest was Bacchus, the wine deity (see illustration, opposite).

No festal god was dearer to Roman hearts than Saturn (see page 112), whose annual celebration in December, the Saturnalia, was in many ways a precursor of the modern Christmas. Originally celebrated on the seventeenth of the month, the festivities later stretched over the better part of a week. In Rome itself, the

LEFT **A Roman calendar fragment with a profusion of festival days marked. Toward the end of the Empire, almost half the total number of days in the year were allocated to the recognition of state festivals. This staggering figure had serious economic implications, for no work was allowed on feast days, except from the slave labor force.**

festival began with a sacrifice in Saturn's temple in the Forum, followed by a public feast open to all comers. Thereafter, the festive season was a time of general goodwill in which the usual social norms were overturned. The most solemn senators wore casual tunics in place of formal togas, and there was even some cross-dressing. Slaves were treated as members of the household. Public gambling, normally strictly prohibited, was permitted, and households often appointed a mock king who acted in the spirit of the medieval Lords of Misrule.

Gifts were exchanged and feasting complemented the general merriment: the traditional seasonal repast was suckling pig. The festival came to occupy such a prominent place in Roman hearts that Christian leaders in the fourth century CE chose to co-opt it for their own purposes rather than to ban it as a relic of paganism. Neither the Bible nor early tradition recorded the date of Christ's birth, but its celebration in late December became accepted, partly in order to preserve the festive mood of the Saturnalia in Christian guise.

RIGHT **Bacchus, god of wine, is depicted in this head of bronze with silver inlays (1–50CE)—note the twisted ivy in his hair, an evergreen plant associated with Bacchus. The head probably once formed part of a large statue. The orgiastic rites associated with Bacchus's Greek counterpart, Dionysus, were introduced to Rome late in the 3rd century BCE by Greek and Etruscan prisoners of war, but proved too depraved for the order-loving Republic to tolerate. They were banned by the Senate in 186BCE.**

GODS OF THE PROVINCES

Formulaic and state-oriented as it was, Rome's public religion commanded citizens' patriotism more than their devotion. People had to look elsewhere to find faiths that satisfied their deeper needs. As the nation's military power increased, a growing tide of foreigners reached Italy, whether as merchants or as prisoners of war, bringing with them new gods that better suited these urges. Eastern and Egyptian beliefs helped fill a gap at the heart of Roman life—one that was ultimately to be satisfied by the triumph of Christianity.

At first, Greek and Etruscan deities helped flesh out Rome's own shadowy and insubstantial divinities. From the late third century BCE on, however, more exotic cults made their influence felt. A crucial step was taken in the year 204, when Hannibal's army had been occupying Italy for well over a decade. Following advice from the Delphic oracle and the Sibylline Books (see pages 128–129), the Senate made the momentous decision to bring the cult statue of Cybele from its home in Asia Minor to Rome. The oriental goddess subsequently became known to Romans as the Great Mother (*Magna Mater*). The stone image made the journey in state, accompanied by five *quinqueremes* (galleys with five banks of oars), and was solemnly welcomed to the Temple of Victory on the Palatine Hill. With Cybele, to the Romans' disquiet, came her priests, the *galli*, who performed ecstatic dances and self-flagellation. Worse still, they castrated themselves in honor of Cybele's consort, Attis, who had

LEFT **The cult of the solar divinity Mithras had widespread support among the Roman legions from the end of the 1st century BCE until the 3rd century CE. The cult operated in great secrecy —worshippers gathered in a Mithraeum, an underground sanctuary, and the faith's teachings were revealed only to male initiates. The Mithraeum shown here lies beneath the church of St. Clemente and is one of more than 40 shrines dedicated to the worship of Mithras that have been found in Rome.**

supposedly emasculated himself in a fit of madness. The Senate looked upon such un-Roman activities with alarm, and Roman citizens were long banned from participating in the rites.

From Egypt came the worship of Isis. For the most part, Romans regarded the various animal-headed Egyptian deities with a mixture of incredulity and scorn, but the Hellenized cult of the goddess and her husband-brother Serapis (as Osiris became known under the Ptolemies) was a different matter. With its stately rituals conducted by shaven-headed priests and its emphasis on loving kindness and female fecundity, the faith appealed strongly to women. In later times, images of Isis cradling the infant Horus in her arms influenced Christian iconography, paving the way for the cult of the Virgin and Child.

Mithraism, which also left its mark on early Christianity, could hardly have been more different. It was aggressively masculine—only men were allowed to attend its services, which were held in small underground sanctuaries. The focus of the faith, which came originally from Persia, was Mithras, a sun god who had sacrificed a bull at the start of time to bring life to the world. Bull sacrifice continued to play a part in the cult, which preached the spiritual equality of all believers and spread initially among slaves brought as prisoners of war from Asia Minor. In time, Mithraism, which stressed comradeship and loyalty and offered various stages of initiation for the faithful, became deeply entrenched among the military and traveled across the Empire with the legions. But its appeal, based on what would now be called male bonding, was intrinsically limited—in the long run, it lacked the all-embracing attraction of the Christian message of universal compassion.

LEFT In addition to Mithraism, Asia Minor was also the center of the exotic cult focused on the goddess Artemis, whose most famous shrine was at Ephesus. This bronze and alabaster statue of the goddess is a 2nd-century CE Roman copy of an older eastern original. Under the peace of Rome, Ephesus once again flourished in the eastern Aegean and became the leading city in the province of Asia, aided in part by the pilgrim trade focused on Artemis. A huntress, Artemis was the equivalent of the Romans' Diana.

THE VILLA OF THE MYSTERIES

In 1909, archaeologists investigating a villa on the outskirts of Pompeii uncovered an extraordinary mural that led the house to be called the Villa of the Mysteries. The painting stretched around all four sides of a windowless room. Scholars think that it was painted in the middle of the first century BCE—the time of Julius Caesar.

There is less agreement as to what its almost-life-size figures depict, but the consensus is that they show an initiation into the Dionysian mysteries, imported from Greece into Italy as the cult of Bacchus. A reclining male figure occupying a central position facing the room's entrance is identified as Dionysus by his *thyrsus*—a staff entwined with vine leaves and ivy that was symbolic of the god. He lies against the lap of a partly obscured female figure, probably his mother Cybele. The other images are more enigmatic, although the two groups flanking the god on either side are generally taken to show crucial moments in a Dionysiac initiation rite. In a detail from the north wall reproduced here (right), the messenger of the gods, Silenus, is shown playing a lyre while three woman appear to be preparing a table.

The Bacchic rites had been banned in Italy in 186BCE, more than a century before the mural was painted (see page 120). It seems likely that they survived clandestinely, particularly in the south, where Greek influence was strong. The villa may have been a meeting place for followers of the proscribed cult, and the room may well have witnessed rituals modeled on those that its walls record.

TEMPLES AND SHRINES

Temples were the main centers of the state religion in the Roman world, but they were not the only ones. Many ceremonies and festivals took place out of doors, and there were also small roadside shrines where the *lares publici*—state or city household gods (see pages 118–119)—could be worshipped. Usually these altars were placed at crossroads, a throwback to earlier times when similar sanctuaries had been set up at boundary points between landholdings (see page 119).

Roman temples did not function in the same way as churches, synagogues, or mosques do today, in the sense that there was no routine of regular worship attracting congregations. Instead, they served as symbolic homes for the gods, who were represented by statues and tended by priests who, in the higher echelons at least, were elected officials chosen from the ranks of the ruling classes. These individuals carried out the formulaic rituals whose regular performance was deemed essential to ensure divine goodwill. Ordinary people might visit the temples, but only as petitioners seeking favors. Typically, they would burn incense and then stand with arms upraised to pray for the benevolent intercession of the resident deity, perhaps to cure an illness or to help in a business transaction or a love affair.

Early temples were relatively plain though dignified buildings, based on Etruscan models. They were typically raised on platforms and were accessed by steps from the front. Inside, a long room lined by columns would lead the eye to a statue of the god or goddess. In later times, at least in Rome and other major cities, these effigies were often splendidly carved in marble, painted in bold colors, and adorned with gold, silver, and gems.

LEFT **The city-state of Gerasa in Roman Syria (modern-day Jerash, Jordan) contains extensive freestanding ancient Roman ruins. The city reached its height in the 2nd century CE, flourishing on trade with the Nabaeans. At this point, a reconstruction program was undertaken and its large Temple of Artemis was constructed (dedicated in 150CE), its columns seen here looming above the ruins of the early Christian church.**

The buildings performed other functions besides their religious use. All true temples had been consecrated by augurs (see page 128; the English word "inaugurate" commemorates this custom), and so were considered to be divinely sanctioned for the conduct of important public business; for example, the Senate frequently met there. They also served as museums for works of art looted abroad by the imperial armies, particularly from Greece.

Oddest of all to modern sensibilities, temples functioned as banks. From early on, they were used to house the state treasury, and the custom continued at least into late republican times; after crossing the Rubicon and marching on Rome, Caesar had to threaten to kill the guards of the Capitoline temple before he could gain access to its wealth. Private citizens similarly took advantage of the security provided by the main state sanctuaries to deposit their valuables.

DIVINATION AND ORACLES

Convinced as they were that the gods had powers to influence human destiny, the Romans spent much effort working out what their will might be. A college of augurs, elected for life from the ranks of the ruling class, sought divine guidance by taking the auspices before important decisions were made. The process usually involved scanning the sky for omens in the form of flights of birds—their species, numbers, and direction could all be significant. Alternatively, the augurs studied the feeding patterns of chickens, especially before military ventures. There were several tales told of commanders who had failed to carry out the necessary observances and paid dearly for their temerity.

The Senate, along with many private individuals, also turned for advice to the soothsayers known as *haruspices*, who practiced the skill the Romans called "the Etruscan science." Usually it involved examining the entrails of sacrificial animals, most often sheep or oxen; the shape, size, condition, and markings of the liver and gall bladder were considered particularly significant. The *haruspices* also took note of omens in the form of monstrous births or growths—two-headed calves and the like—and of lightning, seen as a message from the gods. The best remembered of all soothsayers was Spurrina, the Etruscan who famously warned Julius Caesar to beware the Ides of March. According to the historian Suetonius, who tells the story, Caesar chided him minutes before his assassination, saying that the Ides of March had come. "Come, but not yet gone," Spurrina muttered presciently.

Other valuable sources of information about the divine will were the Sibylline Books, preserved in a vault under the Temple of Jupiter

BELOW The "Fegato di Piacenza" ("Liver of Piacenza"), an Etruscan bronze representation of a sliced sheep's liver, unearthed in Piacenza, Italy, in 1877, and dating from the 1st century BCE. The liver is inscribed with the names of Etruscan deities and is thought to have been used by *haruspices*, or soothsayers, to foretell the future.

RIGHT The rock-hewn tunnel leading to the cave in the acropolis hill near Cumae where the legendary Sibyl was believed to have lived. When the original Sibylline prophecies were destroyed by fire in 83BCE, the Senate sent envoys to Greece to find replacements, for antiquity preserved the memory of several different prophetesses of that name. The substitute pronouncements evidently also proved efficacious, because they continued to be used late into the imperial period, with the last recorded consultation taking place in 363CE.

on the Capitoline Hill. These venerable documents purportedly contained oracular pronouncements of the Sibyl, a legendary prophetess who had once inhabited a cave at Cumae, near Naples; in the *Aeneid*, Virgil makes her Aeneas's guide for the descent to the Underworld. The books, which were said to have been purchased by Tarquinius Superbus, the last Etruscan king, were consulted in times of emergency; it was partly on their advice that the cults of Cybele and of the healing god Aesculapius were brought to Rome from the Orient.

THE TRIUMPH OF CHRISTIANITY

One of the great, abiding mysteries of Roman history is the way in which Christianity, long regarded as a bizarre, antisocial, and possibly dangerous cult, rose from persecution to become the official religion of the Empire in the course of the fourth century CE. The turnaround was nothing if not sudden. In 303CE, the emperor Diocletian launched the most direct assault the Christian community had yet faced, seeking to extirpate the faith entirely in favor of a revived paganism. Just ten years later, however, a new emperor, Constantine, issued the Edict of Milan, which granted Christians complete freedom of worship. By the end of the century, the emperor Theodosius I had proscribed paganism, forbidden the veneration of the old classical gods, and pronounced Christianity the official religion of the entire Roman Empire.

Christianity's beginnings hardly seemed to promise any such outcome. Jesus was, of course, crucified at the behest of Pontius Pilate, the Roman governor of Judaea, and the stigma of his execution cast a long shadow over the faith in Roman eyes. The religion nonetheless made its presence felt in Rome as early as the emperor Claudius's reign (41–54CE), to judge from comments made by the historian Suetonius, who made note of the disturbances stirred up in the city's Jewish community "at the instigation of Chrestus [sic]"—presumably a reference to disputes that took place between supporters and opponents of Jesus in the years after the Crucifixion. By the time of Claudius's successor Nero, the Christians were well enough established to be brutally persecuted in the wake of Rome's Great Fire of 64CE, for which they were made the scapegoats.

Persecution continued sporadically for the next 200 years. The Christians' fault was twofold in Roman eyes: they were a clandestine organization—always a cause

RIGHT **The interior of a two-story catacomb chamber in the Capodimonte area of Naples, north of the ancient city walls. It is cut from tufa stone and shows fragments of mosaic and fresco decoration dating to around the 2nd century CE. The site was once the tomb of an important pagan family, but it was gradually usurped by Christians for their own burial niches. The Christian takeover was made complete in the 5th century CE when the bones of San Gennaro (St. Januarius) were interred there. The cemetery was active until the 11th century CE, when the bones were moved to ossuaries on the lower level.**

for suspicion—and they refused to participate in the state cult of the classical gods, including that of the deified emperors. Christian intransigence in this respect led to an upsurge in harassment under the emperor Domitian (81–96CE), who insisted on being recognized as "lord and god," a formula that the faithful could not accept. Meanwhile, the underground nature of their worship led to various accusations among the masses, not least of which was that they practiced cannibalism—probably a misunderstanding of the symbolic consumption of Christ's body and blood in the bread and wine of the Eucharist. Many of the early martyrs met their deaths not

at the hands of the imperial authorities, but rather from mobs incensed by rumors or with local scores to settle.

The official attitude for much of this time was one of wary sufferance. When the writer Pliny the Younger was appointed governor of Bithynia on Turkey's Black Sea coast early in the second century CE, he wrote to the emperor Trajan for advice on how to handle the region's Christians. Trajan replied that he should not deliberately seek them out for persecution and should not pay attention to anonymous denunciations, which were "unworthy of our age" (Pliny had received many such). However, Trajan concluded, if Christians were properly identified and convicted, they should be punished.

Attitudes toward Christianity hardened in the third century when Rome came under renewed pressure from the barbarian peoples beyond its frontiers. Rome's rulers responded with increased demands for imperial unity. At the beginning of the century, Septimius Severus banned Christians from baptizing new converts, and, in its middle years, Decius launched the first major drive to extirpate the faith. Christianity's darkest years came between Decius's accession in 249 and 311, when Diocletian's measures were rescinded.

The faith nevertheless survived these trials. Yet it was by no means the only foreign religion competing with the pagan gods for the loyalty of the Roman people. All flourished on the inadequacies of the state religion, with its formulaic rites and all-too-human gods. The mystery religions, including Christianity, offered in contrast an outlet for spirituality, the hope of immortality, and a moral urge born of revulsion at the crass materialism of much of Roman life.

Christianity's rivals, however, all had weaknesses that disadvantaged them in the struggle for the Empire's soul. The eunuch priests of Cybele were ultimately too alien for Roman tastes, as were the animal-headed Egyptian deities that formed a

RIGHT **A Roman flask, 300–400CE, possibly for holy water, decorated with Christian symbols. The Greek name of Christ (*XPICTOC*) was probably the inspiration for the use of the *chi* (X) monogram.**

backdrop to the cult of Isis. Mithraism long provided a serious challenge, but its fatal weakness was that it was limited to men.

In the long run, the most immediate threat to Christianity came from the cult of Sol Invictus, the "Unconquered Sun," which spread across the Empire in the years immediately before its final acceptance under Constantine. This solar faith was compatible with paganism, yet also reflected a monotheistic impulse that paved the way for the worship of a single, all-powerful God. Interestingly, Constantine, Christianity's champion, was said to have been initially won over to the cause by a vision of the cross set over the sun that was accompanied by the words, "Conquer with this." The next stage of his conversion was purportedly a dream that came to him on the eve of the Battle of the Milvian Bridge in 312CE, in which he was instructed to decorate his soldiers' shields with the Christians' Chi-Rho (a monogram of the Greek letters X and P, the first two letters of "Christ" in Greek). His subsequent victory over his chief rival for the imperial throne convinced him to accept the faith and to propagate it, not least by founding Constantinople as a new, Christian capital for the eastern Empire.

The Roman world changed irrevocably with the triumph of Christianity. Although the western Empire still had 150 years to run, and the eastern more than a millennium, the old cultural certainties were gone. A new age was dawning, ushered in by such thinkers as St. Augustine of Hippo who, despite being steeped in the classical tradition, rejected many of its tenets. By the fourth century CE, the Middle Ages were already in the making.

THE END OF EMPIRE

The fall of the Roman Empire is traditionally dated to 476CE, yet few people at the time would have guessed that anything epoch-making had happened. The year saw the enforced abdication of Augustulus, the last ruler of the western Empire, and his replacement as king of Italy by the "barbarian" general Odoacer, of Germanic descent. Yet Odoacer himself was thoroughly Romanized in culture, and he continued to use much of the traditional Roman apparatus of government.

Meanwhile, the eastern half of the Empire survived intact, with its own emperor firmly ensconced in his capital of Constantinople, on the shore of the Bosphorus, where Europe and Asia meet. The eastern emperors conspired actively to regain the western lands, and in the sixth century they temporarily fulfilled their ambition. A great emperor, Justinian, and a brilliant general, Belisarius, combined to win back first Rome's old North African lands from the Vandals who now held them and then Italy, which had been seized from Odoacer by the Ostrogoths. Their triumph was short-lived: within three years of Justinian's death in 565CE, another Germanic people, the Lombards, were pushing deep into Italy.

The Empire's swan song is commemorated in a series of brilliant 6th-century mosaics in the Church of San Vitale in Ravenna, Justinian's Italian capital. Yet, as this detail (right) shows, the atmosphere is already non-Roman. The formality of the poses of Justinian (with a halo to signify his sacred status) and his retinue of officials, soldiers, and ecclesiastical dignitaries suggests a new distance between subject and spectator. The humanism of the classical order has given way to the spiritual, God-centered Christian vision of the Byzantine world.

GLOSSARY

basilica A royal palace; a rectangular building with a broad nave, ending in an apse, and flanked by colonnaded aisles, used in ancient Roman times as a courtroom or public hall, and in the Christian era as a church.

city-state A state made up of an independent city and the territory directly controlled by it.

civic That which belongs to a city or its citizens or pertains to citizenship.

consul Either of the two chief magistrates of the ancient Roman republic.

corruption Evil or wicked behavior; depravity; bribery or similar dishonest dealings.

cosmopolitan Not bound by local or national habits or prejudices; common to or representative of all or many parts of the world; worldly.

decadence A process, condition, or period of decline, as in morals; deterioration; decay.

empire Supreme rule; absolute power, authority, and dominion; government by an emperor or empress; a group of states or territories under the sovereign power of an emperor or empress; a state uniting many territories and peoples under one ruler.

frieze A decoration or series of decorations forming an ornamental band around a room or mantel; a horizontal band, often decorated with sculpture, running across a building's walls.

gladiator In ancient Rome, a man who fought other men or animals with a sword or other weapon in an arena for the entertainment of spectators. Gladiators were slaves, captives, or paid performers.

Hellenistic Characteristic of the thought, culture, ethics, customs, language, history, or character of ancient Greece.

hinterland An area far from big cities or towns; back country; the inland region claimed by the state that owns the coast.

imperial Relating to empire; of a country having control or sovereignty over other countries or colonies; having the rank of emperor or empress; having supreme authority; sovereign; majestic.

infrastructure The basic installations and facilities on which the continuance of a community or state depends, such as roads, schools, bridges, and transportation and communication systems.

legion A military division ranging from 3,000 to 6,000 foot soldiers with additional cavalrymen; a large group of soldiers; an army.

legionnaire A member of a legion.

pastoral Relating to or portraying rural life, especially relating to the rustic life of shepherds and dairymaids; characteristic of rural life, idealized as peaceful, simple, and natural.

patrician A member of any of the ancient Roman citizen families; a member of the nobility.

patron In ancient Rome, a person who had freed his slave but still had a paternal control over him; a protector; a benefactor; a wealthy and influential person who sponsors a person, activity, or institution.

piety Devotion to religious duties and practices.

plebeian A member of the ancient Roman lower class; one of the common people.

prowess Bravery; valor; superior ability and skill.

republic A state or nation in which the supreme power rests in all the citizens entitled to vote and is exercised by representatives elected, directly or indirectly, by them and responsible to them.

villa A country house or estate, perhaps large and luxurious and used as a retreat or summer house.

yeomanry The class of freemen who worked their own small holdings of land; small landowners; an attendant or manservant in a royal or noble household.

FOR MORE INFORMATION

British Museum
Great Russell Street
London, England WC1B 3DG
Tel: +44 (0)20 7323 8299
Web site: http://www.britishmuseum.org
The British Museum's collection of seven million objects represents the rich history of human cultures, including that of ancient Rome.

Metropolitan Museum of Art
1000 Fifth Avenue
New York, NY 10028
(212) 535-7710
Web site: http://www.metmuseum.org
The Metropolitan Museum of Art has recently reopened its renovated and newly installed Greek and Roman galleries, displaying thousands of beautiful masterworks, including stone and bronze sculptures, ceramics, glass, jewelry, wall paintings, and architectural elements. The collection of Greek and Roman art at the Metropolitan Museum—more than seventeen thousand works ranging in date from the Neolithic period to the time of the Roman emperor Constantine's conversion to Christianity in 312 CE—includes the art of many cultures and is among the most comprehensive in North America. The objects in the department range from small, engraved gemstones to black-figure and red-figure painted vases to over-life-size statues. They reflect virtually all of the materials in which ancient artists and craftsmen worked: marble, limestone, terra-cotta, bronze, gold, silver, and glass, as well as such rarer substances as ivory and bone, iron, lead, amber, and wood.

Museum of Fine Arts Boston
Avenue of the Arts
465 Huntington Avenue
Boston, MA 02115
(617) 267-9300
Web site: http://www.mfa.org
The collection of Roman art (1st century BCE — 3rd century CE) is one of the best in the world. It is particularly strong in marble portraiture, coins, gems, and cameos. A remarkably complete group of decorations comes from a villa at Pompeii. The collection of art from the Roman provinces has no rival in the United States. A geographically diverse collection of works from Late Antiquity (4th – 7th centuries CE) illustrates the transition from the Classical world to the Christian culture of the Byzantine Empire.

Peabody Museum of Archaeology and Ethnology
Harvard University
11 Divinity Avenue
Cambridge, MA 02138
(617) 496-1027
Web site: http://www.peabody.harvard.edu
The Peabody Museum of Archaeology and Ethnography is steward to one of the oldest and largest collections of cultural objects in the Western Hemisphere. Since the late nineteenth century, the museum has played an active part in the history of American anthropology and in the evolving relationship between museums and native peoples. The collections continue to grow through by gift, fieldwork, and purchase. Today, the Peabody houses more than six million individual objects, 500,000 photographic images, and substantial archival records. The Peabody is caretaker to important collections from Africa, Europe, and Asia. Collection types include archaeology; ethnography; osteology; and painting, drawing, and prints.

University of Pennsylvania Museum of Archaeology and Anthropology
3260 South Street
Philadelphia, PA 19104
(215) 898-4000
Web site: http://www.penn.museum
The University of Pennsylvania Museum of Archaeology and Anthropology, through its research, collections, exhibitions, and educational programming, advances understanding of the world's cultural heritage. Founded in 1887, Penn Museum has conducted more than 400 archaeological and anthropological expeditions around the world. Three gallery floors feature materials from Egypt, Mesopotamia, the Bible lands, Mesoamerica, Asia, and the ancient Mediterranean world, as well as artifacts from native peoples of the Americas, Africa, and Polynesia.

Yale University Art Gallery
P.O. Box 208271
New Haven, CT 06520-8271
(203) 432-0600
Web site: http://artgallery.yale.edu
Yale's art from the ancient Mediterranean world comprises over 13,000 objects from the Near East, Egypt, Greece, Etruria, and Rome that range in date from the Neolithic through the early Byzantine periods. Recent acquisitions in Greek, Etruscan, and Roman art have concentrated largely on marble sculpture, especially portraits, bronzes, and Greek vases. Yale's collection of ancient glass is among the best in the United States.

Web Sites
Due to the changing nature of Internet links, Rosen Publishing has developed an online list of Web sites related to the subject of this book. This site is updated regularly. Please use this link to access the list:

http://www.rosenlinks.com/civ/rome

FOR FURTHER READING

Angela, Alberto (trans. Gregory Conti). *A Day in the Life of Ancient Rome*. Europa Editions: New York, 2009.

Baker, Simon. *Ancient Rome: The Rise and Fall of an Empire*. BBC Books: London, 2007.

Beard, M.; North, J.; and Price, S. *Religions of Rome*. Cambridge University Press: Cambridge, 1998.

Boardman, John. *The Oxford History of Classical Art*. Oxford University Press (OUP): Oxford, 2001.

Boardman, J.; Griffin, J.; and Murray, O. (ed.). *The Oxford History of the Roman World*. OUP: Oxford and New York, 2001.

Brown, P. *The World of Late Antiquity*. W. W. Norton & Co.: London and New York, 2010.

Carcopino, Jerome. *Daily Life in Ancient Rome*. Carcopino Press, 2008 (new ed.).

Claridge, Amanda. *Rome: An Archaeological Guide*. OUP: Oxford, 1998.

Cornell, T. *The Beginnings of Rome*. Routledge: London, 1995.

Everitt, Anthony. *Augustus: The Life of Rome's First Emperor*. Random House: New York, 2007.

Flower, H.I. (ed.) *Cambridge Companion to the Roman Republic*. Cambridge University Press (CUP): Cambridge, 2004.

Gardner, Jane F. *Roman Myths* (The Legacy Past). University of Texas Press: Austin, 1993.

Gibbon, Edward; Womersley, D. (ed.). *The History of the Decline and Fall of the Roman Empire*. Penguin Classics: London and New York, 2001 (abridged ed.).

Goldsworthy, Adrian. *How Rome Fell: Death of a Superpower*. Yale University Press: New Haven, Connecticut, 2010.

Goldsworthy, Adrian. *In the Name of Rome: The Men Who Won the Roman Empire*. Weidenfeld & Nicolson: London, 2004.

Goodman, M. *The Roman World 44BC–AD180*. Routledge: London, 1997.

Heather, Peter. *The Fall of the Roman Empire: A New History of Rome and the Barbarians*. OUP: Oxford, 2007.

Holland, Tom. *Rubicon: The Last Years of the Roman Republic*. Anchor Books: New York, 2005.

Huskinsson, J. (ed.) *Experiencing Rome: Culture, Identity and Power*. Routledge: London, 2000.

Jenkyns, Richard. *The Legacy of Rome: A New Appraisal*. OUP: Oxford, 1992.

Jones, Peter V., and Sidwell, Keith C. *The World of Rome: An Introduction to Roman Culture*. CUP: Cambridge, 1997.

Livy (trans. Aubrey de Sélincourt). *The Early History of Rome*. Penguin Classics: Harmondsworth, 2002 (rev. ed.).

Meijer, Fik. *The Gladiators: History's Most Deadly Sport*. St. Martin's Griffin: New York, 2007.

Millar, F. *The Emperor in the Roman World*. Duckworth: London, 1992 (2nd. ed.).

Potter, D.S. *The Roman Empire at Bay, AD180–395*. Routledge: London and New York, 2004.

Ramage, Nancy S. and Andrew. *Roman Art*. Prentice Hall: New Jersey, 2008 (5th ed.).

Scarre, Chris. *The Penguin Historical Atlas of Ancient Rome*. Penguin Books: Harmondsworth, 1995.

Stierlin, Henri. *The Roman Empire: From the Etruscans to the Decline of the Roman Empire*. Taschen: Cologne and London, 2002.

Strauss, Barry. *The Spartacus War*. Simon & Schuster: New York, 2010.

Suetonius (trans. Catharine Edwards). *The Lives of the Caesars*. Oxford Paperbacks: Oxford, 2000.

Suetonius (trans. Robert Graves). *The Twelve Caesars*. Penguin Classics, 2007 (rev. ed.).

Syme, Ronald. *The Roman Revolution*. Oxford Paperbacks: Oxford, 2002.

Tacitus (trans. Kenneth Wellesley). *The Histories*. Penguin Classics: Harmondsworth, 1998.

Tripolitis, Antonia. *Religions of the Hellenistic-Roman Age*. W. M. Eerdmans Publishing Company: Grand Rapids, Michigan, 2001.

Virgil (trans. David West). *The Aeneid*. Penguin Classics: Harmondsworth, 2003.

Wells, Colin. *The Roman Empire*. Harvard University Press: Cambridge, Massachusetts, 1995.

Wells, Peter S. *The Battle That Stopped Rome*. W. W. Norton, London and New York, 2003.

Wiseman, T.P. *The Myths of Rome*. University of Exeter Press: Exeter, 2004.

Woolf, Greg (ed.). *Cambridge Illustrated History of the Roman World*. CUP: Cambridge, 2003.

Zanker, P. *Roman Art*. J. Paul Getty Museum: Los Angeles, 2010.

INDEX

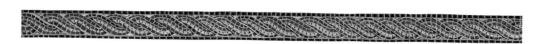

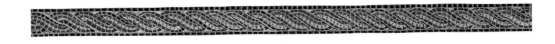

ABOUT THE AUTHOR

After studying History at Oxford University, Tony Allan was for many years a writer and editor with Time-Life Books, serving as series editor of the Time-Life History of the World and working as an author and consultant on *Myth and Mankind*, a 20-volume study of comparative mythology. His own books include *Americans in Paris*, a study of American writers and artists in 1920s Paris, and, for younger readers, *Tales of Robin Hood* and *Ancient China*. He is also the author of *Prophecies*, *The Archaeology of the Afterlife*, *The Symbol Detective*, and *The Mythic Bestiary* (all for Watkins/DBP).

PICTURE CREDITS

The publisher would like to thank the following people, museums, and photographic libraries for permission to reproduce their material. Every care has been taken to trace copyright holders. However, if we have omitted anyone we apologize and will, if informed, make corrections in any future editions.

Abbreviations
c center; l left; r right
AA = The Art Archive, London
BAL = The Bridgeman Art Library, London
BM = British Museum, London
GM = The J. Paul Getty Museum, Malibu, California
MH = Michael Holford, Essex
Scala = Scala, Florence

Page 1 Archaeological Museum, Timgad/AA/Dagli Orti; **3** BM; **6** Museo Capitolino, Rome/AA/Dagli Orti; **7** Kunsthistorisches Museum, Vienna/BAL; **8** Museo Capitolino, Rome/AA/Dagli Orti; **9** Axiom, London/Guy Marks; **10** Provinciaal Museum G.M. Kam te Nijmegen, Nijmegen/AA/Dagli Orti; **11** Museo della Civiltà Romana, Rome/AA/Dagli Orti; **14** Werner Forman Archive, London; **15** BM/MH; **16 c** GM/Bruce White; **16 l and r** GM/Ellen Rosenbery; **17** GM/Bruce White; **18** GM/Ellen Rosenbery; **19** BAL; **21** Scala; **22–23** BAL; **24** Corbis, London; **25** Museo della Civiltà Romana, Rome/AA/Dagli Orti; **27** Whitestar; **28–29** AKG, London/Erich Lessing; **30** AA/Dagli Orti; **31** GM/Ellen Rosenbery; **32** GM/Ellen Rosenbery; **33** GM; **34** Musée National du Bardo, Tunis/AA/Dagli Orti; **35** Museo della Civiltà Romana, Rome/AA/Dagli Orti; **36** Museo della Civiltà Romana, Rome/AA/Dagli Orti; **37** Museo della Civiltà Romana, Rome/AA/Dagli Orti; **38** Kunsthistorisches Museum, Vienna/BAL; **39** Vatican/Scala; **40** AA/Dagli Orti; **42** Kunsthistorisches Museum, Vienna/BAL; **43** GM/Louis Meluso; **44** Israel Museum, Jerusalem/AKG, London; **45** Leslie Garland Photography, Northumberland; **46** Musée du Louvre, Paris/AA/Dagli Orti; **48** Museo Nazionale Terme, Rome/AA/Dagli Orti; **49** Museo Archeologico Nazionale, Naples/BAL; **50** National Museum, Bucharest/

AA/Dagli Orti; **52–53** Museo Nazionale Terme, Rome/AA/Dagli Orti; **54** Museo Archeologico, Venice/AA/Dagli Orti; **55** BM/MH; **56** Fitzwilliam Museum, University of Cambridge/BAL; **57** BM/MH; **58** BAL; **59** BAL; **60** MH; **61** Archaeological Museum, Djemila/AA/Dagli Orti; **62–63** Axiom, London; **65** Museo Archeologico Nazionale, Naples/BAL; **66** Museo Archeologico Nazionale, Naples/BAL; **67 l and r** GM/Ellen Rosenbery; **68** Museo Archeologico Nazionale, Naples/BAL; **69** GM/Bruce White; **71** BM/MH; **72** Museo della Civiltà Romana, Rome/AA/Dagli Orti; **73** National Historical and Cultural Museum, Backchisarai, Crimea/AA/Dagli Orti; **74–75** Museo Archeologico Prenestino, Palestrina/AA/Dagli Orti; **76** Museo della Civiltà Romana, Rome/AA/Dagli Orti; **77** Accademia Italiana, London/BAL; **79** BAL; **80** Villa dei Misteri, Pompeii/BAL; **81** GM/Ellen Rosenbery; **82** AA/Private Collection; **83** Galleria Borghese, Rome/AA/Dagli Orti; **84** AA/Dagli Orti; **85** Musée de la Civilisation Gallo-Romaine, Lyons/AA/Dagli Orti; **86–87** Angelo Hornak, London; **88** Bibliothèque Nationale, Paris/AA; **89** GM/Ellen Rosenbery; **90** Museo della Civiltà Romana, Rome/BAL; **91** Museo Archeologico Nazionale, Naples/BAL; **93** Somerset County Museum, Taunton Castle/BAL; **94–95** Museo Capitolino, Rome/BAL; **97** Magyar Nemzeti Galeria, Budapest/BAL; **98** Museo della Civiltà Romana, Rome/AA; **99** Museo Capitolino, Rome/Scala; **100–101** Musée du Louvre, Paris/BAL; **102** Robert Harding Picture Library, London/Adam Woolfitt; **104** BAL/Alinari; **105** GM/Ellen Rosenbery; **106** Museo Pio Clementino, Vatican/Scala; **107** Museo Capitolino, Rome/Scala; **108** Archaeological Museum, Sousse/AA/Dagli Orti; **109** BM/MH; **110** GM/Ellen Rosenbery; **111** GM; **112** Musée National du Bardo, Tunis/BAL; **113** Vatican/Scala; **114** Museo Nazionale Terme, Rome/AA/Dagli Orti; **115** Museo Archeologico Nazionale, Naples/BAL; **116–117** Angelo Hornak, London; **118** Werner Forman Archive, London; **119** GM/Bruce White; **120** Museo Archeologico, Venice/AA/Dagli Orti; **121** GM/Bruce White; **122** Werner Forman Archive, London; **123** Museo Archeologico Nazionale, Naples/BAL; **124–125** Villa dei Misteri, Pompeii/BAL; **127** Corbis, London; **128** Museo Civico, Piacenza/Scala; **129** Werner Forman Archive, London; **131** Catacombs of St. Janrius, Naples/BAL; **133** BM/BAL; **134–135** San Vitale, Ravenna/BAL.